Learning to Use
Your Bible

THE DISCIPLESHIP SERIES

Learning to Use Your Bible

OSCAR E. FEUCHT

Publishing House
St. Louis   London

The Discipleship Series

A BASIC CHRISTIAN LIBRARY
To Equip Today's Christians
for Their Role as CHURCH

Learning to Use Your Bible
Christians Worship
The Christian's Mission
Christian Family Living
The Church Since Pentecost

These practical, learn-by-doing paperbacks focusing
on the skills of Christian living were written at the direction of the Board of Parish Education of The Lutheran
Church — Missouri Synod

Bible quotations in this study are from the Revised
Standard Version unless otherwise noted.

Concordia Publishing House, St. Louis, Missouri
Concordia Publishing House Ltd., London, E. C. 1
© 1969 Concordia Publishing House
Library of Congress Catalog Card No. 77-76228

MANUFACTURED IN THE UNITED STATES OF AMERICA

Contents

The Discipleship Series

The Christian faith is not a dead or static belief. By its very nature it is dynamic. And we live in a very dynamic world. It has the right to expect the church to fulfill its God-given functions, meeting the needs of men through its members in every context of life.

The church has the commission from its Lord to transmit the true faith as delivered to it by the apostles, and to equip its people for their Christian mission in all walks of life.

Frequently it has taken great pains to pass on the creeds of Christendom and the saving knowledge of Christ, but in many instances without adequately equipping its people for the functions of Christian discipleship.

To meet this need the Discipleship Series has been designed. These paperbacks focus on the skills of Christian living: use of the Bible, the Christian's mission, the Christian family, Christian worship, and an understanding of the church since Pentecost.

The series has been planned in consultation with laymen and ministers. Each book has been field tested.

This study text is designed to be part of a five-book personal library to take its place beside your Bible. For churches wishing to offer a course on each of these vital subjects, a leaders manual for each book has been prepared.

The Board of Parish Education is grateful to all who have helped make this series possible: the test-copy readers, the field-test groups, and especially the editorial committee, Reuben C. Baerwald and Victor A. Constien.

The renewal and strength of today's church is closely related to a functioning laity equipped in Christian discipleship.

OSCAR E. FEUCHT
Series Editor

Preface

It is easy to have and to hold the Scriptures, and easier still merely to venerate the Bible and treat it as a symbol. Although the Bible is the most widely sold book in the world, a great many church people are almost Biblical illiterates or know only fragments of the Scripture. They may be avid readers of magazines, be acquainted with literary masterpieces, and boast that they have read the latest novel or challenging new paperback. Might we not expect Christians to know their way around in the Bible?

There is also much faulty use of the Scripture as people quote passages out of context. Jesus criticized the Pharisees for such faulty use. They found in the Old Testament mainly laws and regulations which they meticulously refined and expanded, and so missed the main message, the promises of the Savior. (John 5:39-43)

One reason for the inadequate and faulty use of the Scripture (apart from the culture of our times) is the fact that few church people have ever read a book which introduces the Bible to them, or taken a course which gives them the "keys" to the Biblical library. That is precisely the purpose of this book.

How can we see the trees without getting lost in the forest? How can we find our way through these 66 books? Is there a thread we can take from Genesis to Revelation? How can we get the full sweep of what God wants to say to us for our generation? For this we need perspective, just as we need a road map to take us over the main highways to our destination. There is unity within the diversity of the Scriptures, and it soon becomes apparent to the careful reader.

But the reader must stand within the Bible. Each person must put himself into the scene. He must come to it in faith and hear God speaking to him. Continually the reader must ask: "What is its meaning for my life?" As he does this he will note that the main message of Scripture centers in what God has done, is still doing, and will do for us men and for our salvation in Jesus Christ.

LEARNING TO USE YOUR BIBLE is a compact study text. It contains many Bible references. They are included not only to support its statements but to give the reader a handling acquaintance with the sacred Scriptures. Skills of Bible use are learned by practice. It is suggested that each chapter be read twice, the first time to get its main thrust and the second time to look up some of the chief references in each section. References shown in parentheses are for further study. The reader's background, Biblical knowledge, and interest should determine this.

The Bible has three purposes: (1) to bring the saving Gospel of Jesus Christ to more and more people, (2) to help those who know Christ to grow in the grace and knowledge of their Lord and Savior, and (3) to equip God's people for their mission in life. Keep these three purposes in mind as you read this book. May it give you a better understanding of its nature and message, new skills for its fruitful use, and a stronger faith in our wonderful God and Savior.

Chapter 1

Personal Use of the Bible

Introduction

Each of the 66 books of the Scriptures has its own message and is part of God's written revelation to man. From a practical point of view, however, we may speak of the Bible as containing three "books": a book of doctrine, a book of worship, and a book to live by. We find instruction or teaching in all of them. We also find some elements of personal or group worship in all of them. And, of course, every book gives us some directions for daily life. Many know the Bible as a book of doctrine and make some use of it as a book of worship. We all have much to learn in making it also a book to live by.

An Oklahoma schoolteacher and her father, before retiring for the night, announced to house guests that it was their habit to begin each day with their private devotions and spend at least 10 minutes thinking of the work to be done during the course of that day. They used this period to let the light of Scripture fall upon their daily task, asking God for His guidance and blessing upon their labors.

George Mueller of Bristol, England, attributed his spiritual vigor to his devotional use of the Bible. He made it a point to spend a half hour in prayer each day, but soon noticed that his praying became repetitious and shallow. Then he discovered that after the first 15 minutes of Bible reading he was richly fed with new thoughts—thoughts which he then included in his prayers. You too can enrich every day of your life by daily Bible reading and prayer.

The famous Bible teacher and evangelist Dwight L. Moody once said: "A man can no more take in a supply of grace for the future than he can eat enough for the next six months, or take sufficient air into his lungs at one time to sustain life for a week. We must draw upon God's boundless store of grace from day to day as we need it."

I. Taking God into Our Lives

Being a Christian is more than knowing the doctrines of Christianity. It is knowing God Himself as He has revealed Himself in Jesus Christ. We discover what being a Christian is from Ephesians 3:16-19: power through the Spirit; Christ making His home in our hearts; our lives rooted in God's love; being filled with the fullness of God.

In the Bible we are to "encounter" God; come face to face with our Creator and Lord. When the Lord and His prophets and apostles use the word "hear," they mean more than hearing words with the auditory nerve. They mean: listen and understand, accept and respond in your heart and life. We are to *know* God personally and deeply as He knows us. In Bible reading we are to have a *confrontation* with God!

Life with God includes "practicing His presence." That means being conscious that in God we live and move and have our being. One of the purposes of the Scripture is to let God come into our lives. We begin the day, live each hour of it, and close it with God. Consciously or unconsciously we live as in His presence. We worship Him not only when we read and pray but also when we serve people in Christ's name, because God lives in our heart.

We all know people who live comparatively barren lives. Their days are drab. To them life seems purposeless, unchallenging, and without spiritual adventure. This does not mean that they are idle but that their lives are all wrapped up in social functions, political life, business enterprises, and the quest for happiness and success. But God is missing. God is not in any of their thoughts. (Psalm 10:3-4 KJV)

Must we not also admit that at times we all lose spiritual poise and Christian purpose because we allow the things of this world to hide God from view like clouds hide the sun? We let fears displace hope and darkness shut out light. Instead we can have the light and power which Paul prays for and be the new creation which God has made us in Christ.

12

The God of our Lord Jesus Christ, the Father of glory . . . give you a spirit of wisdom and of revelation in the knowledge of Him, having the eyes of your hearts enlightened, that you may know what is the hope to which He has called you, what are the riches of His glorious inheritance in the saints, and what is the immeasurable greatness of His power in us who believe, according to the working of His great might which He accomplished in Christ when He raised Him from the dead and made Him sit at His right hand in the heavenly places. *Ephesians 1:17-20*

If any one is in Christ, he is a new creation; the old has passed away, behold, the new has come. *2 Corinthians 5:17*

Life in the Spirit produces love, joy, peace, patience, kindness, goodness, faithfulness, gentleness, and self-control (Galatians 5:22-23). In His Word Christ gives to our lives strength and purpose.

Life in today's world is more complex than ever. Operating a business, managing a household, and "keeping up with the Joneses" put the whole family in a whirl. Radio and television programs can enrich us. They also can intrude upon our privacy. We try to find an outlet in sports or entertainment, but none of these things are really satisfying. They do not re-create the spirit of man. In this kind of hustle-and-bustle world spiritual meditation is not a luxury but a necessity. We all find time to eat three meals a day and even waste considerable time in useless, almost unprofitable conversation. But do we provide an opportunity for God to make us strong in our inner selves? (Ephesians 3:16)

Bible reading is not an exceptional thing for the literate Christian. It is part of his response to God. By hearing, reading, studying, and thinking about God's Word we have encounter with God. The devotional life consists of two parts: (1) God speaking to us in public worship, in family and personal Bible reading, and (2) we responding to God in prayer, praise, and thankful living, not only on Sunday but every day.

Each Christian, however, must take the initiative. "In a church service you can be a spectator. Someone else is organizing and operating the service. You can become involved if you desire, or you can just sit back and watch. But in your personal devotional periods you are the pastor, the organist, and the choir, in addition to being the congregation. Here you cannot be a spectator. Either you plan and lead the worship, or there is no worship." (Dale S. Bringman and Frank W. Klos, *Prayer and the Devotional Life*, p. 113)

Establish a time each day for the Word of God and prayer and you will find greater meaning and depth for living.

> Everything created by God is good, and nothing is to be rejected if it is received with thanksgiving; for then it is consecrated by the Word of God and prayer.
>
> *1 Timothy 4:4-5*

II. How the Bible Helps Us

Psalm 23 is unequaled for its strengthening power. It has been called the nightingale of psalms. One writer has correctly said: "It has charmed more griefs to rest than all the philosophy of the world. It has remanded to their dark dungeon more wicked thoughts, more black doubts, more thieving sorrow than there are sands on the seashore. It has comforted the noble host of the poor. It has sung courage to the army of the disappointed. It has poured balm and consolation into the hearts of the sick, of captives in their dungeons, of widows in their pinching griefs, of orphans in their loneliness. Dying soldiers have died easier as it was read to them; ghastly hospitals have been illumined. It has visited the prisoner and broken his chains." (F. W. Herzberger, *Family Altar*, 1964 ed., p. 125)

Millions of Christians know this psalm and have used it hundreds of times because it brings God so near. Yet it is only one of the great passages of Scripture which speak to our many spiritual needs.

Bibles, hymnbooks, reading guides, and devotional manuals sometimes include a list of Biblical texts especially chosen to enrich our devotional life. Some of these daily readings guide us through the festival and nonfestival seasons of the church year. The ancient reading lists give us readings not only for Sundays but for every day of the year. There are many kinds of lists. At the close of this chapter four general lists supply helpful references on:

Christian Doctrines
Practical Guidance
Help in Time of Need
Christian Discipleship

Practice: As you read these lists, check one or two items in each of the four categories that are related to your own or your neighbor's felt need; read the passages; then ask yourself: "How does this Scripture help me?"

No list, however large, can exhaust the great classical passages of the Old and New Testaments. Every Christian in the course of his life makes his own selections of great passages. You will constantly be discovering more of them. Many Christians find that their Bible use is more rewarding when they look for —

A Thought for the Day

In the personal use of the Bible we look for a guiding directive for the day. Sometimes we may read a whole chapter and not find something personal or striking. Again we may find a thought peculiarly fitting in almost every paragraph. The gospels are filled with such statements, for instance:

Whoever seeks to gain his life will lose it, but whoever loses his life will preserve it. *Luke 17:33*

This verse is a call from Christ to put Him first in your life. You pause a minute to fix the verse in your heart. You think about it. You grasp its meaning. The person who is constantly concerned only with the saving of his physical life and his earthly goods will lose forever the true life.

Time and again through the day this verse comes back to you to help you keep your Christian sense of values, to put the highest price tag on the things of the Spirit. It helps you cultivate the inner self — the life of the soul. This verse has also a wider application. You put your mission to others in Christ's name ahead of your own convenience. You help someone in the office with his work. You use your lunch hour to call on someone who is ill. The Word of

Jesus helps you in hundreds of ways to seek first the kingdom of God and His righteousness.

Tomorrow find another verse that speaks to you pointedly and gives you "God's marching orders" for the day. In this way find *a thought for each day* of your week in a single chapter. Now practice this procedure by finding *a thought for the day* in James 1.

Help in Time of Need

The Bible is timeless. It fits every age. It is always relevant. It has a word for us in every situation — for times of joy and celebration (Psalm 103), for times of great trial and decisions (1 Peter 1:3-9), for times of great physical danger, distress, or anxiety. (Psalm 91)

Modern man is often beset by problems that overwhelm him and bring him to the brink of despair. None of us is completely free from *fear*. In such moments we can get help from such verses as Isaiah 41:10 and

> The Lord is my Light and my Salvation; whom shall I fear?
> The Lord is the Stronghold of my life; of whom shall I be
> afraid? *Psalm 27:1*

Like Peter, we all have times when faith is faint and we need our Lord's outstretched hand (Matthew 14:31). When *worry* overtakes us, we can get a new view of ourselves as creatures of God by reading:

> What is man that Thou art mindful of him, and the son of
> man that Thou dost care for him? Yet Thou hast made him
> little less than God, and dost crown him with glory and
> honor. Thou hast given him dominion over the works of
> Thy hands; Thou hast put all things under his feet.
> *Psalm 8:4-6*

Then there are such passages, like Psalm 94:19 and 1 Peter 5:7. When *death* takes a believing member of the family or a friend from us, we get superhuman help from John 10:27-28; 11:25-26; 14:1-6. Consider also these words:

> For this is the will of My Father, that every one who sees
> the Son and believes in Him should have eternal life; and
> I will raise him up at the last day. *John 6:40*

These are only a few examples of how Scripture speaks to us personally in every situation and gives us a life-giving Word.

III. Christ and His Word Sustain Us

A person can be "lost" in his own community, an outcast and a vagabond, counting the world a mistake and life not worth living; or he can be a person convinced that the world in which he lives is the Father's house where he is a welcome child. The person who puts God into the very center of life and lives with this conviction finds a security that only faith can supply.

Man is what he thinks in his heart. If the heart is wrong, nothing can be right. But if the center of life is sound, the whole being will have health. In Luke 11:33-36 Jesus uses an illustration to prove this point: An eye with clear vision is compared to an eye that has lost vision. Speaking in our day Jesus might have used the shutter of a camera for an example.

Christ alone gives us real security and life. Those who find Him have life abundantly here and hereafter (John 10:10). They have the peace that passes all understanding, the wisdom that comes from heaven, the character that the Holy Spirit imparts, and a mission in life that is unsurpassed. They say with Paul: "The life I now live in the flesh I live by the faith of the Son of God, who loved me and gave Himself for me" (Galatians 2:20). Nothing shall separate us from the love of God which is in Christ Jesus, according to Romans 8:39. "It is no longer I who live, but Christ who lives in me" (Galatians 2:20). "I know whom I have believed and am persuaded that He is able to keep that which I have committed unto Him against that day" (2 Timothy 1:12 KJV). Such people can meet life unashamed and unafraid because they have unfaltering faith in an unfailing God.

Christ is the Bread of life (John 6:35). He is also the Water of life, saying: "If anyone thirst, let him come to Me and drink" (John 7:37). Then He adds the promise: "Out of his heart shall flow rivers of living water" (John 7:38). With Peter such a person will say: "Lord, to whom shall we go? You have the words of eternal life." (John 6:68)

Jesus could feel the hunger of man, and so He fed the multitudes with fishes and bread. But knowing that man doesn't live by bread alone, He provided Word and sacraments for the spiritual needs of man.

St. Augustine spoke for all generations when he wrote: "Thou hast made us for Thyself, and our hearts are restless until they rest in Thee." Thousands have had the experience that nothing else will satisfy when once a person has seen and accepted Jesus Christ.

> Jesus, Thou joy of loving hearts,
>   Thou fount of life, Thou light of men,
> From the bliss that earth imparts,
>   We turn unfilled to Thee again.

FOR FURTHER STUDY

Books in the Discipleship Series deal with *functional Christianity*, that is, with the *practice of our faith*. Each chapter is followed by suggestions for getting further *experience* in some skills. This book deals with the *use* of the Bible. Bible use, like piano playing, can be learned only by *practice*. The reader is therefore encouraged to learn the Christian art of Bible use and so enrich the rest of his life by following the daily readings. One author speaks of such readings as "daily minimum spiritual vitamins."

MEDITATIONS ON THE LORD'S PRAYER

(1) Each day read Martin Luther's explanation and related Scripture, (2) apply the petition to yourself by using the questions and (3) pray.

Sunday **Our Father who art in heaven.**

First Petition Here God encourages us to believe that He is truly
Luke 11:1-13 our Father and we are His children. We therefore are to pray to Him with complete confidence just as children speak to their loving father.

Hallowed be Thy name.

God's name is hallowed whenever the Word is rightly taught in its truth and purity and we as children of God live in harmony with it. Help us to do this, heavenly Father! But anyone who teaches or lives contrary to the Word of God dishonors God's name among us. Keep us from doing this, heavenly Father! Read the Bible passage. Ask yourself: When and where have I been irreverent toward God? misused His name? neglected His Word? been slipshod in my church attendance? Continue with such questions, thus personalizing the petition. Then make a short prayer asking God for greater love and reverence toward Him and a greater sense of His presence every day.

Monday
Second Petition
Matthew
13:31-52

Thy kingdom come.

God's kingdom comes when our heavenly Father gives us His Holy Spirit, so that by His grace we believe His holy Word and live a godly life on earth now and in heaven forever.

Read one of the Kingdom parables in Matthew 13. Then ask yourself: What hinders the kingdom of God from coming more fully into my life? Is it selfishness? pride? intolerance? weakness of faith? Ask God in prayer for the gift of the Holy Spirit, for a stronger faith, for a clearer understanding of His Word.

Tuesday
Third Petition
Luke 22:39-53

Thy will be done on earth as it is in heaven.

God's will is done when He hinders and defeats every evil scheme and purpose of the devil, the world, and our sinful self, which would prevent us from keeping His name holy and would oppose the coming of His kingdom. And His will is done when He strengthens our faith and keeps us firm in His Word as long as we live. This is His gracious and good will.

Read the story of Jesus in Gethsemane. Why did Jesus set so high a goal "as it is done in heaven"? What is God's will for me this day with regard to my family relationships? my occupation and calling? my needy neighbors? my schooling and Christian growth? my church relationships? Ask God to help you get a clearer understanding of His will and provide the faith humbly to obey it in all areas of life.

Wednesday

Fourth Petition
1 Timothy
2:1-8

Give us this day our daily bread.

Daily bread includes everything needed for this life, such as food and clothing, home and property, work and income, a devoted family, an orderly community, good government, favorable weather, peace and health, a good name, and true friends and neighbors.

Read the Bible selection. Then note how broadly Luther interprets "our daily bread." The original may be translated "give us day by day our daily bread." What does this imply? Whom should you cherish more than you now do in your family and relationship? among your friends? among your neighbors? Let your prayer now grow out of a deeper sense of thanksgiving for food and clothing, friends, good government, and thank God for giving you this attitude toward people and things.

And forgive us our trespasses, as we forgive those who trespass against us.

Thursday

Fifth Petition
Luke 7:36-50

We ask in this prayer that our Father in heaven would not hold our sins against us and because of them refuse to hear our prayer. And we pray that He would give us everything by grace, for we sin every day and deserve nothing but punishment. So we on our part will heartily forgive and gladly do good to those who sin against us.

What does Luke 7 teach about forgiveness? This calls for confession of the things you have not done but should have done, of the things you did which you should never have done, of attitudes that are sub-Christian, of secret thoughts which are displeasing to our Lord. Tell God how sorry you are. Ask for His forgiveness and accept it, because it is the first step toward renewal of life. Meditate on the words "as we."

How forgiving have you been this day? Whom have you forgiven?

Friday

Sixth Petition
Matthew
4:1-11

And lead us not into temptation.

God tempts no one to sin, but we ask in this prayer that God would watch over us and keep us so that the devil, the world, and our sinful self may not deceive us nor draw us into false belief, despair, and other great and shameful sins. And we pray that even though we are so tempted we may still win the final victory.

Read the story of Jesus' temptation. Frankly face your own temptations. Are they spiritual coldness? overindulgence? lustful thoughts? hypocrisy? thoughtlessness toward others? Then ask God to give you victories for today by the power of the indwelling Spirit and to make you strong against temptation.

Saturday

Seventh Petition
Romans 11:33–
12:2

But deliver us from evil.

We ask in this inclusive prayer that our heavenly Father would save us from every evil of body and soul, and at our last hour would mercifully take us from the troubles of this world to Himself in heaven.

For Thine is the kingdom and the power and the glory forever and ever. Amen.

Amen means "Yes, it shall be so." We say Amen because we are certain that such petitions are pleasing to our Father in heaven and are heard by Him. For He Himself has commanded us to pray in this way and has promised to hear us.

How does the Scripture selection relate to the whole Lord's Prayer? In your hymnbook thoughtfully read the hymn "Praise to the Lord, the Almighty, the King of Creation." Make it fully your own expression of praise to God for what He has given you in the created world about you, in the gift of His Son Jesus Christ, and through the enabling power of His Holy Spirit. (Adapted from *The Awakened Heart*)

References

Bringman, Dale S. and Frank W. Klos. *Prayer and the Devotional Life.* Philadelphia: Lutheran Church Press, 1964.

Kettner, Elmer A. *A Closer Walk with God.* St. Louis: Concordia Publishing House, 1959. 95 pp.

————. *Living with My Lord.* St. Louis: Concordia Publishing House, 1961. 76 pp.

Stackel, Robert. *The Awakened Heart.* Philadelphia: Muhlenberg Press. Pp. 73—75.

Young, Henry. *Bible Reading Guide.* Minneapolis: Augsburg, 1958. 96 pp.

Basic Christian Doctrines

How God has revealed Himself — Ps. 19; 2 Tim. 3:15-17; John 1:1-18.
God and His chief creation, man — Gen. 1—2; Ps. 139.
Man's relation to God — Ex. 20:1-11; Matt. 4:10; Matt. 22:37.
Man's relation to man — Ex. 20:12-17; Rom. 13:8; Matt. 22:39.
Man's failure — sin — Gen. 3; Eccl. 7:20; Rom. 3:23.
Christ made us right with God —
   Rom. 5; Rom. 3:23-25; 1 Peter 1:18-19; John 14:6.
Christ earned for us new life — here and hereafter —
   John 10:10; John 3:16, 36.
Salvation through faith in Christ by the Holy Spirit —
   Rom. 3:25-28; Eph. 2:1-10; Gal. 2:16; John 3:5-6.
Fellowship with God through Baptism —
   Gal. 3:26-27; John 3:5-6; Acts 2:38-39.
Fellowship assured and proclaimed in the Lord's Supper —
   Matt. 26:26-28; 1 Cor. 10:16-17; 11:23-25.
Talking with God in prayer — Acts 2:42; John 16:23; James 5:13-18.
Walking with God in the Christian life —
   John 15:5, 16; 2 Cor. 5:17; Eph. 2:10.
Working with God in the church and in the world —
   Matt. 28:18-20; Acts 1:8; 8:4-8.
Being faithful to God, avoiding what endangers faith —
   Rev. 2:10; 2 Cor. 6:14-18.
The church: fellowship in the body of Christ —
   Eph. 2:19-22. Rom. 12:4-5.

Practical Guidance

Marriage and divorce — Matt. 19:3-9.
Christian home relations — Eph. 5:21 — 6:4.
Employer-employee relations — Col. 3:22 — 4:11.
Christian fruitfulness — John 15.
Christian gifts and their use — 1 Cor. 12; Rom. 12.
The priesthood of all believers — 1 Peter 2:1-10.
Christian witnessing — Matt. 28:18-20; John 17:15-20; 20:21.
Christian stewardship — 2 Cor. 8 and 9; 1 Cor. 16:1-2.
Christian love and service — 1 Cor. 13; John 13:34-35; Mark 10:44-45.

Help in Time of Need

Comfort in time of sorrow — John 10, 11, and 14.
Relief in time of suffering — Heb. 12:3-13; 2 Cor. 12:8-10.
Guidance in time of decision — James 1:5-6; Prov. 3:5-6.
Protection in time of danger — Ps. 91; Ps. 121.
Courage in time of anxiety — Ps. 27; Heb. 13:5-6; Eph. 6:10-18.
Peace in time of turmoil — Is. 26:3-4; Phil. 4:6-7.
Rest in time of weariness — Matt. 11:28-29; Ps. 23.
Strength in time of temptation — James 1:12-16; 1 Cor. 10:6-13.
Warning in time of indifference — Gal. 5:19-21; Heb. 10:26-31.
Forgiveness in time of penitence — Is. 1:18; 1 John 1:7-9.

Christian Discipleship

Faith — John 2:11; Acts 16:31.
Love — John 13:34-35.
Growth — John 8:31-32; Mark 9:31.
Self-denial — Luke 14:27, 33; Matt. 10:24-25.
Followership — Matt. 9:19.
Fruitfulness — John 15:8.

Chapter 2

The Bible and Your Devotional Life

Martin Luther was a very creative man. His many sermons, books, Bible studies, hymns, and tracts have amazed everyone. His great productivity was closely related to a strong personal faith. He once revealed that the secret was spending sufficient time to feed his soul every day by reading and meditating on God's Word.

Once Peter the barber asked Luther for help in developing his devotional life. The Reformer took time to write a 30-page booklet on meditation for Peter. Luther said in effect: I take a verse or petition or commandment of Scripture and reflect on it. As I do so I soon find in it *instruction* for my personal faith and life; and this in turn prompts me to *thanksgiving*. As I reflect further on the verse and find that I have come short of what God requires, I am led to penitent *confession*. This is followed by *petition* in which I ask God for new strength to believe, to be, and to do what the passage has taught me. As I read God's Word I hear the Holy Ghost speaking to me; and when He teaches me, I keep silent and become His student. In this manner I find in each verse four "intertwined wreaths." One I name "instruction," another "thanksgiving," a third "confession," and a fourth "petition." — You too will find this to be a simple formula for devotional Bible reading.

Like Luther, millions of Christians today have devotional practices. They make it part of their daily living to let God speak to them, and they respond to God, not only in prayer but in the way they live. This is evident in the lives of Christian students, housewives, day laborers, machinists, brokers, bankers, real estate salesmen. God goes with them into every day. He lives in their hearts. They invite Him in by letting the Word of Christ dwell in them. (Colossians 3:16-17)

I. The Art of Meditation

Webster defines meditation as "a spiritual exercise consisting in deep continued reflection on a religious theme." When we meditate, "we relax and let God take over." We give ourselves completely to Him. We let God draw our thinking toward Himself.

Meditation has been called thinking with a view to planning and action. Meditation is defined in such passages as Psalm 4:4, "Commune with your own hearts"; Psalm 19:14, "Let the words of my mouth and the meditation of my heart be acceptable in Thy sight, O Lord, my Rock and my Redeemer."

One of the chief benefits of a Christian retreat is giving people an opportunity to be by themselves, read the Word, engage in prayer, and have time enough to rethink their lives in the light of God's will. In meditating we permit the Holy Spirit to talk to us. We have dialog with God. The thoughts of God are communicating with our own thoughts. Where God's Word is in use, God Himself is at work.

The word "meditate" is used very frequently in the Old Testament, especially in the Psalms. Jeremiah speaks of eating the Word of God: "Thy words were found, and I ate them, and Thy words became to me a joy and the delight of my heart, for I am called by Thy name, O Lord, God of hosts" (Jeremiah 15:16). The Scripture is a table richly laden with spiritual food.

Devotional Bible use is not unlike digesting food. By chewing, food is mixed with digestive fluids. Then it is turned into blood sugar that supplies energy for living. Meditation does for us spiritually what eating does for us physically.

Meditation is a very personal thing. You bring your needs and concerns to God. God in turn speaks to you. It may be a word of condemnation and judgment or a word of grace and forgiveness. In the process a feeling of penitence is created, faith and hope are renewed, and new encouragement and direction are given for Christian living and service.

Discover the different words used to describe meditation in Psalm 77:3, 6, 11-12.

What do each of the following passages tell you about meditation?

Joshua 1:8: "This Book of the Law shall not depart out of your mouth, but you shall meditate on it day and night, that you may be careful to do according to all that is written in it; for then you shall make your way prosperous, and then you shall have good success."

Psalm 1:2: "His delight is in the law of the Lord, and on His law he meditates day and night."

Psalm 63:5-6: "My soul is feasted as with marrow and fat, and my mouth praises Thee with joyful lips when I think of Thee upon my bed and meditate on Thee in the watches of the night."

Psalm 143:5: "I remember the days of old, I meditate on all that Thou hast done; I muse on what Thy hands have wrought."

On the basis of these passages, how would you define "meditate"?

PRACTICE

Meditate on one or more of the seven "I am" statements in John's Gospel, and write in your key thoughts.

John 6:35 _____

John 8:12 _____

John 10:7 _____

John 10:14 _____

John 11:25 _____

John 14:6 _____

John 15:5 _____

II. Four Simple Steps for the Devotional Use of the Bible

1. The Approach

Go to your selected Scripture passage *expectantly*, looking for the message God wants to give you. "They who seek, find," said Jesus. Approach it with a prayer, for instance, with the words of Psalm 119:18, "Open my eyes, that I may behold wondrous things out of Thy law," or with the words of 1 Samuel 3:9, "Speak, Lord, for Thy servant hears."

The Christian approach to the Scripture is one of reverence.

It is a posture of submission and of faith. It stands ready to obey Christ (2 Corinthians 10:5). Pray for the guidance of the Holy Spirit, for it is He who is promised to every Christian as his Teacher and Enlightener (John 16:12-15). Our Lord has promised that the heavenly Father will give us the Holy Spirit, if only we ask. (Luke 11:13)

But the Counselor, the Holy Spirit, whom the Father will send in My name, He will teach you all things and bring to your remembrance all that I have said to you.

John 14:26

2. The Inquiry

All Scripture is profitable, but in various ways. It has many messages for us. Look for the meaning for yourself. The Sacred Writings are profitable for salvation, instruction, judgment and correction, restoration and forgiveness; for a God-pleasing life of righteousness; and to fit us out for good works of every kind. (2 Timothy 3:14-17)

Reading the Bible is not unlike reading a letter from a loved one. Put your own name into the verse. Most Scripture is just that personal. *As you read, ask yourself: What is the Lord giving me here?* Is it instruction or warning? Is it a call to repentance? to faith? to mission? Is it a promise? guidance? encouragement? Most every passage will give you one of these. Ask God to guide you to some definite thought for yourself. As you examine the passage, you will find a sin to confess, forgiveness in Christ to apply, an example to follow, a promise to claim, an error to avoid, a new thought about God, a new concern for your neighbor, a new purpose for your day.

3. The Prayer

Out of your reading (God speaking to you) should come *a responsive prayer* (you speaking to God). Bible reading has been called "the other side of prayer." As Luther pointed out, the message you receive will suggest thanksgiving, confession, petition, intercession, and the rededication of self to God and to the service of men. Thank God for the directive He has given you, and pray for the Holy Spirit's power to put it to work in your life.

4. The Action

No Scripture is fully received until it is understood and put to work in your life. Paul's encounter with Jesus came to its climax when he asked: "Lord, what wilt Thou have me to do?" (Acts 9:6 KJV). As you read, ask yourself: What am I to know? What am I to believe? What am I to be? What am I to do? Meditation helps us make a passage personal and practical. Until we see its relevance for ourselves we have not yet crossed the bridge from the world of the Bible to the world of today.

In meditation we *personalize* and *internalize* the Word God gives. What we *internalize* is to be *externalized*, that is, put to work in our lives. A little girl when asked what translation of the Bible she liked best answered, "My mother's translation," meaning the Bible she saw illustrated in the life of her mother.

PRACTICE

Selecting *one* of the following passages, follow the four steps outlined above. In a notebook write down your thoughts as you apply the passage to your life.

Mark 2:1-5, 11-12
John 14:1-4
John 20:21
2 Corinthians 5:17-20a
Galatians 2:15-20
Colossians 1:9-14

III. Getting Started

Christian discipleship involves certain Christian disciplines. The Gospel is not a law that commands. It proclaims the free grace of God. It creates a desire to keep in communion with God in Christ. Love driven by faith causes the Christian to accept such disciplines as mealtime prayers, family or personal devotions, worshiping with the Christian congregation on Sunday, setting aside a portion of his income for the spread of the Gospel, and dedicating his talents and abilities to the service of the church and mankind.

It is from this perspective that the Christian is willing also to set aside a definite time for the devotional use of his Bible. He may begin by working through a gospel, using psalms or hymns as he finds them related to his daily Bible reading. Many Christians have decided to read a chapter a day. It will not be necessary to meditate on each verse or pick up every thought, but at least one verse of the chapter should be used for special reflection and response.

Meditations turn spiritual food into the energy, tenacity, zeal, and ardor of the Spirit. As we meditate, "we find the ability to pray with sincerity, the wisdom to arrive at right decisions, and the toughness to resist temptation," says Robert W. Stackel. He compares meditation to the gardener working plant food to the roots of his favorite rosebush. Meditation works God's truth down deeper into the soul.

We are all tempted to go through our devotions perfunctorily: to read the brief Scripture verselet, say a prayer, and be on our way. Those who stop to think and to relate the verse to "this day" and "my life" will be immensely rewarded.

Of course, it is not easy, just as writing is not easy for a 6-year-old. But once he learns it, he could become an author. Every Christian owes it to himself to acquire this practice. And the humblest, even those with a meager or no education, have learned it.

What we need is both desire and persistence until we have established a habit. But it must not become mere routine. There is a difference between regularity and doing a thing merely from a sense of duty. Let us do it with joy, looking forward to it with zest and anticipating a new discovery each day. The Holy Spirit will not disappoint us. Some days, of course, we will be mentally dull and pressed for time, and then we will get less. Other days the Holy Spirit will open up one new thought after another to deepen our lives and equip us for greater service.

Some Testimonials

A housewife having learned the procedure said, "Now good portions of the Bible are mine, and Bible reading is a pleasure." Persons taking a course on devotional Bible reading gave these testimonies: "This course gave me a key to the Scriptures. Now there is a real purpose for me to read the Bible." "It has helped both my Bible reading and prayer life. I find I can now commune with God more intimately, more personally." "Since taking this course I find much more in the Bible than ever before. I am only sorry I wasn't taught how to read the Bible devotionally as a child. It has enlarged my life." Thousands testify that it has brought them closer to Christ.

Devotional Bible reading is not an escape from the world. It is preparation to meet the world of today with its heavy demands on our time, energies, and inner reserves. It is necessary to avoid boredom and hopelessness, to keep our spiritual equilibrium in a complex society, to maintain God's sense of values in a rapidly changing world. Modern man, instead of needing the practice of devotional Bible reading less, actually needs it more!

FOR FURTHER STUDY

Sunday Acts 16	This week's reading will be in the Epistle to the Philippians. To better understand the situation in Philippi (in Macedonia, Greece), first read about Paul's experiences there on his first visit (Acts 16). Meditate on such verses as 9, 14, 25, 30-31, 34.
Monday Philippians 1:1-11	Discover the kind of relationships which existed between the apostle Paul and the Christians at Philippi: confidence, partnership. What goals for the Christian do you find here? Find in this section instruction, thanksgiving, confession, and petition (Luther's approach to meditation).
Tuesday Philippians 1:12-30	What do you learn here about Paul's spirit? progress of the Gospel? the apostle's high commitment? What are the applications with regard to your purpose for living? Use the four steps: approach, inquiry, prayer, action.
Wednesday Philippians 2:1-30	How is Christ's "servant concept" presented? His humiliation and exaltation? For what purpose does Paul introduce this? Do you see the place of discipline and example in your Christian development? Follow the four steps.
Thursday Philippians 3:1-11	Note here the autobiography of Saul (3:4-6 – before conversion) and of Paul (3:7-11 – after conversion). Do you find a parallel in your own life? Why is this such a powerful lesson on justification by faith? Follow the four steps.

Friday *Philippians* *3:12 — 4:3*	What instructions and incentives do you find here for growth to Christian maturity? What lessons for a congregation to be a "heavenly colony" (v. 20) in its community? Follow the four steps.
Saturday *Philippians* *4:4-23*	Reread the entire letter and underscore every reference (nouns, verbs, adjectives) to Christian joy. Find the secret of Paul's spiritual radiance and power. Pray for this same radiance in your own life.

References

Great men and women of God have left as their heritage what we call the devotional classics: John Gerhard's *True Christianity*, Bernard of Clairvaux's *The Love of God*, Thomas a Kempis' *Imitation of Christ*, St. Augustine's *Confessions*.

Modern examples of devotions growing out of Scripture meditation are many. We list a few by way of examples.

Bash, Ewald. *Seven Days*. St. Louis: Concordia Publishing House, 1966. 101 pp.

Coates, Thomas. *The Psalms for Today*. St. Louis: Concordia Publishing House, 1957. 118 pp.

_____. *The Proverbs for Today*. St. Louis: Concordia Publishing House, 1960. 116 pp.

_____. *The Prophets for Today*. St. Louis: Concordia Publishing House, 1965. 115 pp.

Connell, Marguerite. *Hope for Today* (Scripture selections). Chicago: Moody Bible Institute, 1965. 47 pp.

Kretzmann, O. P. *The Road Back to God*. St. Louis: Concordia Publishing House, 1935.

Preus, J. C. K. *God's Promises and Our Prayers*. Minneapolis: Augsburg, 1961. 158 pp.

Prokop, Phyllis Stillwell. *Conversations with Prophets*. St. Louis: Concordia Publishing House, 1966. 75 pp.

Youngdahl, R. K. *Live Today*. Philadelphia: Fortress Press, 1959. 366 pp.

Chapter 3

How to Read the Bible

Introduction

A lawyer asked Jesus: "Teacher, what shall I do to inherit eternal life?" Jesus answered: "What is written in the Law? How do you read?" (Luke 10:25-26). Our Lord expected His hearers to know the Scriptures! The apostles were at home in the Old Testament. Stephen the Martyr summarized the whole Book of Exodus on a moment's notice (Acts 7). The Bereans searched the Scriptures daily to test the teaching of Paul. (Acts 17)

The writings of the church fathers in the first four centuries make it clear that the early Christians were well grounded in the Old Testament Scriptures. They regarded firsthand knowledge of Scripture necessary to get conviction and to advance in the Christian life. "Teach your children thoroughly the Word of God ... and place in their hands every book of Holy Scripture." (*Apostolic Constitutions*, beginning of the fifth century A. D.)

The Holy Spirit operating through the Holy Scriptures gave Martin Luther his Christian convictions. Luther studied them, translated them, preached them, paraphrased them in his hymns, and summarized them in the Catechism. All his teaching and preaching revolved around the orbit of God's revealed truth. From that time on he was the instrument of God, and the Reformation became God's work.

When Luther and the other reformers insisted on Bible reading for all Christians, they only returned to the simple confidence of the early church. Jerome, who translated the Bible into Latin, wrote, "Ignorance of the Scripture is ignorance of Christ." William Tyndale, one of the greatest English translators, said, "It is impossible to establish the laity in the truth of God unless the Scripture is plainly laid before them."

The Bible is in a class by itself. It has been read and distributed to more people than any "best seller" ever written. It has influ-

32

enced more lives than any other book. It is both disturbing and comforting, controversial and peace-giving, because it finds us where we are, awakens a sense of sin, and declares to us the forgiveness of God in Christ. Millions testify that it is the means by which the grace of God has reached their heart. From every country experiences of this kind could be cited to show that the Word of God gives wings to the spirit.

I. Why Read the Bible

Clarence Smith was a worker in the post office. His little girl enrolled in a Sunday school and invited him to go to church with her. He refused. But when he saw her tears, he consented to go. Christ found him through the spoken Word. Clarence accepted an invitation to join a Bible study group. He began to ask questions, and this led him to reading, to understanding, and to further growth. "It was the turning point in my life," he said. He did more than to become a good student. When his congregation asked him to lead a home-study group, he was thankful for the opportunity. He said, "I guess nobody can do his best for the Lord unless he gets to be a daily Bible reader."

Jesus said: "Man shall not live by bread alone" (Matthew 4:4), and millions of people have learned the truth of this assertion. The Word, spoken or written, is the means of our rebirth (2 Peter 1:19; 1 Peter 1:23-25). Referring to the Gospel, Jesus said: "If you continue in My Word, you are truly My disciples, and you will know the truth, and the truth will make you free" (John 8:31-32). "I commend you to God and to the Word of His grace, which is able to build you up," said Paul to the elders at Ephesus (Acts 20:32). Throughout the New Testament there is a call not to remain babes in our Christianity but to become grown men and women. (1 Peter 2:2; 2 Peter 3:18; Ephesians 3:14-19)

Luther called Psalm 119 the A-B-C of Bible use. In the first nine verses you will find seven expressions which set forth the many aspects of God's written revelation. It is called law, testimonies, precepts, statutes, commandments, ordinances, and 35 times the term "word" is used. The revitalizing power of God's Word is expressed in such terms as "blesses" (v. 1), "keep pure" (v. 9), "confirms" (v. 38), "gives life" (v. 50; KJV, "quickens"), "makes wise" (v. 98), "gives understanding" (vv. 98-99, 105), and "great peace" (v. 165). This longest chapter in the Bible rings with the call: Use the Word of God. Read it. Heed it. Lay it upon your heart. Make it a part of your life.

But is the Bible for modern man? Man's knowledge of his environment is expanding rapidly. He has harnessed the power of the atom. He can photograph galaxies 6 billion light years away. He can land packages on the moon. Yet modern man is also frustrated and confused, searching for meaning for his own life in the universe. Man continues to be his own most vexing problem. It was the famous psychologist Carl Jung who said that the troubles of man are not due to the nature around him but to himself. Why? Because man suffers from a broken relationship to God. (Genesis 3)

But God in Christ has made wholeness of life possible again (John 1:18). He provides relief from a sense of guilt which psychiatry alone cannot provide. God can take away our emptiness. He is the answer to our search for security. There is no Gospel in humanism, scientism, or naturalism. Turning to the Word of his Creator, man finds help for his deepest needs. Modern man needs spiritual power. The more atomic power man is asked to control, the greater is his need to act responsibly to both God and his fellowman.

Bible reading centers our life on God. When done in faith, it becomes a daily expression of our relationship to Christ. The Gospel provides spiritual power and develops Christian maturity.

You may be convinced that you should read the Bible, and even have guilt feelings because you neglect to do so. Your problem may be that no one has really shown you how to read the Bible. It is not easy reading. It is a whole library of books, written over a space of about 1,500 years and telling of God's mighty acts for man's salvation.

II. How to Read the Bible

By Units of Thought

For our convenience the Bible has been divided into chapters and verses. These divisions were not part of the original text.

Sometimes they separate what should remain united. However, not the verse or sentence but the paragraph should be the chief unit in Bible reading. One of the important benefits of modern translations is that many of them arrange the text by paragraphs and sometimes give paragraph subheadings (Phillips, Today's English Version, New English Bible). Most King James editions give some but fewer paragraph signals. Examine the paragraphing, for example, in John, chapter 1.

A paragraph is a unit of thoughts that naturally belong together. The verses of a paragraph should be read and understood together. After finishing a paragraph, summarize it in your own words—the way you would say it today. We call this paraphrasing. This will help you capsule the thought of the writer.

Whole chapters sometimes need to be read together because they form one larger division of thought. The story of Abraham or of Joseph forms such a longer unit of reading.

Often a single verse gives us new light for our life and spiritual food for a whole day. However, the basic rule remains: To get the total message of a book, we need to see it as a whole. Reading by paragraphs is essential for this purpose.

Various Kinds of Reading

Most people do various kinds of reading. Some articles in the newspaper we only scan. Especially meaningful articles we may read more carefully. We may even read them a second time to get their full meaning. Some sections of the Bible (genealogies and historical sections, for instance) need mainly to be scanned in order to get an overview, unless one is reading for some specialized purpose.

At different times we have different purposes in reading Scripture. You may want to get the main stream of thought in a quick survey. You may wish to learn what it says on a certain doctrine or subject. At another time try reading until a new or major thought comes from God to you. Then stop there and meditate on it.

Many people have very profitably read the Bible from Genesis to Revelation, following the rule of three chapters on every weekday and five on Sundays to complete the reading in a year. This can be very beneficial, but it can also become very routine and artificial when the reader makes no distinction between the different types of messages he is reading. Not all parts of the Scripture are of equal value or significance for today.

Some ways of reading the Bible are not to be recommended; for instance, reading the Bible at random, reading it without a purpose, or simply selecting the first passage that meets the eye. This borders on the superstitious. It tears verses out of their context and fragmentizes the Scripture.

It is good to mark the verses which have especially helped us. But when we select only favorite verses, we may be passing by God's words of judgment that call us to repentance, and His words of admonition that call us to improvement of life.

There is no one-and-only way to read the Bible. Christians have discovered many ways and special clues to better understanding. One of these is to find the key word in a chapter or book. Yet, not every chapter has a "key word." In your reading of Philippians you discovered "joy" and "rejoice" as keynotes of the whole letter. "Love" is the key word of John 13 and of 1 Corinthians 13. "Faith" is found 24 times in Hebrews 11.

The New Translations Help

Since 1946 many new English translations of the whole Bible or parts of it have appeared. In the English-speaking world the King James Version, completed in 1611, has become a classic. Increasingly, however, it failed to communicate adequately to the younger generation, chiefly because of changed word meanings. In *The Bible Word Book* (1960) Bridges and Weigle trace the changes in meaning of over 800 English words since 1611. For example, in the 1611 translation "prevent" means "precede," "communicate" means "share," "conversation" means "behavior," "take thought" means "be anxious."

The new translations are helpful because they use words we understand and simpler sentence structures to give the sense of the original Hebrew (Old Testament) and Greek (New Testament). Some of the more widely used newer translations and dates of first appearances are:

Revised Standard Version (1946 New Testament, 1952 Old Testament)
A New Testament in Plain English (C. Kingsley Williams, 1949)
The New Testament in Modern English (J. B. Phillips, 1960)
The New English Bible (New Testament, 1961)
Confraternity Version (Roman Catholic, 1941 New Testament, 1955 Old Testament)
The Berkely Version (1959)
The New Testament in the Language of Today (Wm. F. Beck, 1963)
Today's English Version (*Good News for Modern Man*, 1967 New Testament)

Familiar passages frequently take on added meaning when we read a new rendering of the Scriptures. Compare the following translations of Romans 1:17:

King James Version — "For therein [in the Gospel] is the righteousness of God revealed from faith to faith, as it is written, The just shall live by faith."

Beck — "It reveals God's righteousness as being by faith and for faith, as the Bible says, *By faith you are righteous and you will live.*"

Phillips — "I see in it God's plan for imparting righteousness to men, a process begun and continued by their faith. For, as the Scripture says: The righteous shall live by faith."

NEB — "Here is revealed God's way of righting wrong, a way that starts from faith and ends in faith; as Scripture says, 'he shall gain life who is justified through faith.'"

TEV — "For the Gospel reveals how God puts men right with Himself: it is through faith alone, from beginning to end. As the Scripture says, 'He who is put right with God through faith shall live.'"

New translations speak to our generation in the language of our times. They are bridges to meaning and have ushered in a greater use of the Bible.

Where Begin?

While there is no one place where everybody should begin,

those reading the Bible for the first time would probably do best to begin with the Gospel of St. Luke and follow with the Book of Acts. Here they meet that Person and those events which mark the turning point of human history. The Gospel they proclaim has set countless men and women, youth and children free from fear and shame and sin and brought them to a radiant and abundant faith and life.

In the light of these two books, which present so clearly (1) the message and (2) the mission of the Christian, you will better understand all the other books of the Bible and, in fact, your own life. Add to these two books the Gospel of John and the Letter to the Christians at Rome and you have that combination of books which the American Bible Society has named "The Inside Story."

Because the Bible contains such wide variety, each person will need to decide what he should read next. Here is one suggested sequence: (1) Having read Luke and Acts, move on to some of the shorter letters of Paul; (2) then read Genesis, followed by Exodus, Leviticus, and Numbers; (3) proceed to the Letter to the Hebrews and see how it connects the New Testament with the Old; (4) next get acquainted with the Psalter and some chapters in Proverbs; (5) turn again to the New Testament for another gospel—Matthew, Mark, or John; (6) now turn to one or more of the Minor Prophets, such as Amos and the great Book of Isaiah; (7) then read other letters of the New Testament and the Book of Revelation.

The Book of Psalms meets our devotional needs. Here are prayers, offering of praise, and other expressions of faith: for instance, adoration (Psalms 95, 67), trust and hope (27 and 121), petition (107), repentance (32, 51), festival psalms (95 − 100), historical (107, 114), Messianic (2, 18, 22, 69, 110), God's Word (19, 119). In reading the Psalms and adapting them to our lives and time, we need to put ourselves in the situation of the writer.

Put Yourself into the Scene

Come to your reading with an open mind. Give God a chance to speak to you. The Bible is not simply a record of historical events. It is a message from God to give you light for your life. In reading Scripture it is always good to "put yourself into the scene." Enter into the living experience which it records or relate it to a similar incident in your life.

III. A Reading Plan

Many churches help their members by suggesting various plans and giving adequate motivation. One church of 1,350 communicant members has 628 committed daily Bible readers. It offers various plans:

— a chapter-a-day plan (reading lists supplied)
— readings in the daily devotional booklets (*Portals of Prayer*, etc.)
— the plan of reading through the Bible in a year

Choose a time and place that fits into your personal and family schedule. An attorney following a Bible-reading plan confesses: "I now read something in the Bible every day. When our church's assigned readings got me to reading Proverbs, I found that these Old Testament sayings were practical instructions for everyday living." An office secretary says: "I always wanted to read the whole Bible, but I didn't do it until the year I used 'Through the Bible in a Year' guide." An engineer and Sunday school teacher reported: "I appreciate the daily assignments, and to date I have read 31 of the 66 books of the Bible." A housewife testifies: "I usually read the Bible at a set time every day, and listening to God speak to me through His Word always sets me up for the day." A high school student said recently: "When I read the New Testament, I think of Jesus, and I know He loves me."

IV. Time to Read

The housewife has routines for getting the meals on the table, washing the dishes, and for other daily housekeeping chores. The businessman has a schedule for opening the mail, writing letters, and meeting customers. Every worker must have a routine if he is to accomplish something. Also for Bible reading we need the routine of a regular time, the discipline of a daily rendezvous with God through His Word. Make it what it should be: a joyful and revitalizing experience.

The Bible is a library conveniently broken down into 66 books. Of these, 33 can be read in from 10 to 45 minutes. One of the most beautiful stories ever written is in the Book of Ruth. It takes about 18 minutes to read its four chapters. Most of Paul's letters contain six chapters or less. If we discipline ourselves, we can easily read through the New Testament once a year and pick up important sections of the Old Testament as well, thus getting a broader base for our faith.

Modern man has allowed himself to be too occupied with his work, business, television, sports, and part-time interests. The Christian, however, regards Bible reading and daily worship as part of his style of life. So he arranges for them. *Actually it is always a matter of taking time for the things we want to do.*

> Let the Word of Christ dwell in you richly as you teach and admonish one another in all wisdom and as you sing psalms and hymns and spiritual songs with thankfulness in your hearts to God. And whatever you do, in word or deed, do everything in the name of our Lord Jesus, giving thanks to God the Father through Him. *Colossians 3:16-17*

More important than time is having the right motive and the desire for daily communion with God.

Hearing Sermons Is No Substitute

A lifetime of listening is not long enough to learn the Bible. Relying only on hearing takes a wonderful memory besides. The written Word supports the spoken Word. The book remains when the voice has died away. In reading, you can see a verse again and again. You can weigh every word. No other book will yield so much to the reader as the Holy Scriptures.

Every Christian should be taught to feed himself. It is a great event in a family when a child has learned to handle spoon and fork. The quicker you learn to feed your spiritual life with the Word of God, the better. The more you nourish yourself, the *richer* you will be, the more *useful* you will be, and the *surer* you will be. This will be so if you read in faith and make Christ the object of your Bible reading, namely,

to see Him more clearly,
to love Him more dearly,
to follow Him more nearly, and
to serve Him more sincerely.

It was Luther who said: "Truly, my dear Christians, you cannot *read* too much in the Scripture; and what you read you cannot read too *attentively;* and what you read attentively you cannot *understand* too well; and what you understand you cannot *teach* too well; and what you teach you cannot *practice* too well."

FOR FURTHER STUDY

Do circumstances control Christians, or do Christians control circumstances and set up their own style of life? The Holy Spirit living in our hearts does change our goals and way of life. The pace of modern life need not deprive you of reading the Bible. The suggested readings for the week will show you how rewarding such daily readings can be.

Sunday	How does each of the following passages relate to Christian discipleship: Matthew 4:4; John 8:31-32; Acts 20:32; 1 Peter 2:2-3; 2 Peter 1:19; 3:18? Meditate on each verse.
Monday	Psalm 119 refers to the Word of God heard and read. As you read it in your Bible, underscore (1) the various terms used for God's Word (Law, precept, etc.) and (2) the words which describe its power and joy in the believer's life. Notice how Psalm 119 is paragraphed according to the 22 letters of the Hebrew alphabet. Some Bibles show these letters.
Tuesday	Read Acts 17 by paragraphs, and in your notebook give a title to each paragraph.
Wednesday	Read the four short chapters of 2 Timothy, and enter into your notebook a title for each chapter.
Thursday	Compare the translations of Romans 12:1-2 in KJV, Phillips, RSV, NEB, TEV, or such modern translations as you have at hand. What new insights did they give you? Which helped you get the most meaning?

41

Friday	Read the three short chapters of the Epistle to Titus. Name its paragraphs. What does it say to you personally? to the church of our day?
Saturday	Write out a Bible-reading plan and a schedule for yourself for the next month, using insights gained from this chapter.

References

Bratcher, Robert G., tr. *Good News for Modern Man: The New Testament in Today's English Version.* New York: American Bible Society, 1966. 600 pp. Paperback. $ .35.

————. *Why So Many Bibles?* (available from Concordia Publishing House). 44 pp. Brief but scholarly evaluation of modern English translations. $ .25.

Love, J. P. *How to Read the Bible.* New York: Macmillan, 1959 rev. $3.95.

Reference Edition, American Bible Society's King James Version, 1962. Contains alternative readings and lists for over 500 words that have changed meaning since 1611.

Young, Henry. *Bible Reading Guide.* Minneapolis: Augsburg, 1958. 96 pp.

Chapter 4

How to Study the Bible

Every Christian should know his Bible better than any other book. Once he learns how to study it, he finds it one of the most rewarding experiences of his life, for the Bible is a rich mine that yields its treasures to everyone who is willing to read it seriously.

Can modern Christians get excited about studying the Bible? There is a new concern throughout Christendom in lay Bible study. Roman Catholic educators are saying that we must help Christians deal with the life-giving Word of Scripture itself to understand the worship forms used in the church and to give meaning to the teachings of the catechism. "God's Word is timeless, given for our spiritual instruction at all ages to the end of the world," says one of their leaders. "God not only talks to us; His very Word contains the living power of grace: correction, warning, pleading, consolation, understanding, and love." (Olivier Beguin, *Roman Catholicism and the Bible*)

Yet many church members remain spiritual paupers. They have only a passing acquaintance with the Scripture, largely received as children, and have not continued their Biblical education. Growth and achievement in any field demand serious study. We wouldn't think of stopping short of a high school education, and many of our sons and daughters go on to college. Why expect to be mature Christians without diligent, well-planned, and lifelong Bible study?

In this chapter we are to deal with the *study* of Scripture. The difference between reading and study is like the difference between drifting in a boat and rowing toward a destination. In study we observe carefully the entire structure of a book, the progression of thought, its relation to other books of Scripture, what new insights it gives, and its contributions to our spiritual development.

Bible study, of course, can become something akin to the study of ancient history, namely, merely storing up a lot of facts and

43

becoming acquainted with a world that no longer exists. But this is not really Bible study. *Studying the Bible is crossing the bridge from the world of the Bible to the world of today.* We must indeed know the message at the time the book was written, but we must also find its permanent message for our time, our world, and our personal lives. As this takes place, we move from mere reading to serious study.

＊ Through good Bible study we learn to see all of life in the light of Christ and His Gospel, get spiritual depth, and prepare ourselves for life's mission. The true power index of the church is not to be found in its clergy but in the life and witness of its millions of members. The biggest challenge before the church of today is to accept the laity as the working force of Christ in every context of life. *We study the Bible to function better as Christians.*

I. The Functions of Bible Study

Our bodies have functions necessary for life. When these functions cease, we die. Similarly we may speak of the Bible having functions. How many and what kind of functions can you detect in 2 Timothy 3:14-17?

> But as for you, continue in the truths that you were taught and firmly believe. For you know who your teachers were, and you know that ever since you were a child you have known the Holy Scriptures, which are able to give you the wisdom that leads to salvation through faith in Christ Jesus. For all Scripture is inspired by God and is useful for teaching the truth, rebuking error, correcting faults, and giving instruction for right living, so that the man who serves God may be fully qualified and equipped to do every kind of good work. (TEV)

＊ 1. The Bible supplies *content for worship:* personal, family, and congregational. Knowing the Bible helps us understand our hymns, appreciate the liturgy, and follow the sermon. To fully understand the hymn "Holy, Holy, Holy" demands acquaintance with Isaiah 6:1-8. The hymn "Nearer, My God, to Thee" is based on the story of Jacob's ladder. (Genesis 28)

44

2. Knowledge of the Bible prepares us for effective *witnessing* since it gives us both the message and the method for testimony to our Lord and to our faith. Every Christian should be able to give others a Biblical reason for the hope that is in him. (1 Peter 3:15)

3. Bible study keeps new members *growing spiritually.* It strengthens old members, so that they will not become cold and indifferent and take their religion for granted.

> And so, from the day we heard of it, we have not ceased to pray for you, asking that you may be filled with the knowledge of His will in all spiritual wisdom and understanding, to lead a life worthy of the Lord, fully pleasing to Him, bearing fruit in every good work and increasing in the knowledge of God. *Colossians 1:9-10*

> But grow in the grace and knowledge of our Lord and Savior Jesus Christ. To Him be the glory both now and to the day of eternity. Amen. *2 Peter 3:18*
> See also Ephesians 3:14-19.

4. It equips *fathers and mothers* for their influential role as teachers, guides, and examples to their children.

> These words which I command you this day shall be upon your heart; and you shall teach them diligently to your children, and shall talk of them when you sit in your house and when you walk by the way and when you lie down and when you rise. *Deuteronomy 6:6-7*

5. Only as a large number of members of a *Christian congregation* are rooted in Scripture and understand Christian doctrine can a parish develop the capable churchmen it needs for Sunday school teachers, youth and adult leaders.

> You are a chosen race, a royal priesthood, a holy nation, God's own people, that you may declare the wonderful deeds of Him who called you out of darkness into His marvelous light. *1 Peter 2:9*

6. Firsthand knowledge of Scripture can give us the *deeper convictions* necessary for the stewardship of life, the commitment of time, talents, and treasures to the Lord's service.

> I appeal to you therefore, brethren, by the mercies of God, to present your bodies as a living sacrifice, holy and acceptable to God, which is your spiritual worship.   *Romans 12:1*

✳ 7. Bible study develops the kind of *Christian world view* so badly needed in business, industry, politics, and world affairs. It helps us to be the salt of the earth and the light of the world. (Matthew 5:13-16)

✳ 8. Bible study equips us for our *Christian mission in life* "for the work of Christian service, to build up the body of Christ." (Ephesians 4:12)

Let us frankly face the fact that we cannot build a spiritually growing, active, witnessing, and working laity —

>
> if confirmation is "finishing school"
> if education is for children only
> if churchgoing is all there is to "discipleship"
> if you have your religion only to die by
> if mission is for missionaries
> if religion is left up to the pastor

✳
Bible study helps us equip ourselves for functional Christianity. What will be the place of Bible study in your life?

II. Procedures in Bible Study

Serious study of the Bible is within your capacity. If you are a reader of any one of a dozen major periodicals or any serious book, you need have no inferiority complex in approaching the Bible. The Bible is not that difficult. Besides, you have been given the mind of Christ, and the Holy Spirit dwells in you.

> Who has known the mind of the Lord so as to instruct Him? But we have the mind of Christ.   *1 Corinthians 2:16*

It is important, however, that you learn *how* to study the Bible. Without this skill the Bible can remain for you a closed book. With this skill you can get firsthand convictions instead of relying on the results of other men's studies. You become a student rather than just a listener. Like swimming, typing, and piano playing, it needs to be learned. Once you have learned it, you are better equipped to understand the Bible the rest of your life.

How to Read a Book by Mortimer Adler appeared many years ago. It tells us that any serious book needs three readings: one reading to get a general overview, a second to find its main parts, and a third to digest its meaning for you. Study demands a time exposure — not a snapshot!

✳ *First Reading: Get an Overview* ✳

All Bible students have profited greatly from a quick overview of a book and, if it's not too long, from reading it in a single sitting. Ever so many books of Scripture can be read in an hour or less. In this first reading you will learn what kind of a book it is. You ask:

What gives the book its unity?
What is its main subject?
How is it organized?
Is it all story or narrative?
Is it largely instruction in the Christian faith and life?
Would it be classified as recital of history for the encouragement of saints today (Hebrews 11)?

A new kind of thrill awaits you in reading through the whole Gospel of Mark and getting a fresh impression of the ministry of our Lord. You receive one view of the apostle Paul by reading Philippians and a different view of him by reading Galatians. So first get acquainted with the entire book, not trying to remember everything that you read.

✳ *Second Reading: Find the Outline* ✳

You are now ready to read it a little more slowly and get the major divisions, subdivisions, and paragraphs. Here you will frequently read from one chapter to the other without any pause, remembering that originally the Bible was not divided into chapters or verses. At the close you will put down the major divisions as shown in the diagram below. You will note that the purpose of Luke is stated in Luke 1:1-4. You will get the key to the Book of Acts from Acts 1:8. In this way every book gives you the clew to its meaning. By following this clew you get more fully the particular message it wishes to convey.

✳ Next find the structure of the book. In the diagram of Luke's Gospel read the opening and closing verses of each of the four major sections. The diagram of Acts follows the division suggested in 1:8. Again read the opening and closing verses of each section. You may also divide Acts into the ministry of Peter (Acts 1 — 12) and of Paul (Acts 13 — 28). Acts is the story of the extension of the church to Jews and Gentiles.

Example: THE STRUCTURE OF LUKE-ACTS: The Gospel of God for the Whole World

Vol. I (Luke): As taught, lived, and accomplished (through His death and resurrection) by Jesus of Nazareth				Vol. II (Acts): As spread throughout the Roman world by the witnessing of Jesus' followers		
CHAPTERS				CHAPTERS		
1 — 2 Preparation — Births of John the Baptist and Jesus	3:1 — 9:50 In Galilee	9:51 — 19:27 On the way to Jerusalem	19:28 — 24:53 In Jerusalem	1:1 — 8:3 In Jerusalem	8:4 — 12:25 In Judea and Samaria	13:1 — 28:31 To the end of the earth

✳ *Third Reading: Make It Your Own* ✳

In your third reading of Acts you may wish to trace on a map the three missionary journeys of Paul and note their significance for the spread of the Gospel. Mark and study especially the clear confessions of faith and the testimonies to Christ. What really was the message of the Gospel as they proclaimed it? Find in this book a call to mission. Discover directives for your own life. Underscore verses which refer to the activity of the Holy Spirit. Pray for His presence in the church of our day — and in your life.

✳ Finding the key words of a book is helpful: "faith" in Romans and Galatians; "grace" in Ephesians 1 and 2; "love" in 1 Corinthians; "works" in James. These key words are like the piers of a bridge. Once you understand them, whole "spans" of a book become more meaningful. Alvin Bell's *The Gist of the Bible* is very helpful at this point.

You may not understand everything even in this third reading. There will be some questions you will want to ask, some problems on which you will need more light. A short introduction to the book giving historical background, time and place, information about the author, and a synopsis will help you. You will find such background information in any good introduction to the Old and New Testaments. Study Bibles like *Holman Study Bible*, *The Oxford Annotated Bible*, and *Harper's Study Bible* provide these introductions at the beginning of each book.

There Is No Substitute for Study

By studying the Bible we add to our "spiritual working capital." Just as a businessman can expand his business if he has enough working capital, so a Christian can enrich his own life and increase his service to people as he intimately knows and uses what he has gained from his study. We can perhaps never fully master the Scripture, but we can become so well acquainted with a number of its books that we are always drawing on what they have taught us. Through study they become our own. What Goethe said of culture and earthly values is true also of spiritual values: "What you have inherited from your fathers you must personally acquire to possess." Bible study is the process of personally acquiring the rich heritage of the Christian faith.

III. Three Basic Questions

We must let the Bible speak for itself. True Bible study leads into the Word, not away from it. It submits to the Word of God and doesn't impose its opinion upon it. The purpose of Bible study is to find out: What does the Bible mean for us, here and now? But there are two prior questions: What does it say? and What does it mean?

1. What Does the Passage Say?—Observation

Keen observation of the text itself is of first importance. This

49

is not as simple as it seems, because the text we use is a translation. So you may wish to check other versions. This is necessary when the meaning at first reading is not clear. Often there are different ways in which the meaning of a passage can be given.

Take time to observe what the passage _really_ says. Note what it does _not_ say. This takes sharp observation. Our greatest temptation is to pass by this basic step. If we misread the text, we distort the message. In this sense the Bible student is like a scientist. He is looking for all the observable phenomena or facts.

❋ 2. What Does the Passage Mean? — Interpretation

This asks us to consider the passage in the light of its purpose, subject matter, background, time, and culture. We can determine this by asking: What did it mean to the man who wrote it? What did it mean to those who received it? What circumstances called forth this passage? (The problems which occasioned the writing of Galatians, for instance.) What is the cultural-historical setting? What is the literary form of the passage? Is it poetic imagery? a parable? prose or straight narration? Here the introduction to the particular book in an annotated Bible or a Bible-study guide is helpful.

What does the passage mean in its immediate setting (the book, chapter, paragraph)? What does it mean in the light of the New Testament? the Old Testament? the whole Bible? This step is important! We must know what it meant _then,_ if we would know ❋ what it means _now._

❋ 3. What Does the Passage Say to Us — to Me? — Application

This is really what we want to know. _Now we are crossing the bridge from the world of the Bible to the world of today._ We are moving from the life of the Bible character to our own lives. The message of the Bible has been called "eternally contemporary." There is no book so relevant to all of life, in all ages, and at every age level. We cannot let the Bible alone, because it does not let us alone.

As we study the Bible, we are to let it judge us as the prophets judged Israel. We are to let it absolve us as Nathan offered God's forgiveness to sinning David. We are to accept our new freedom under God's grace as the Galatian Christians did. We are to take up our commission to witness as the 12 apostles did (John 20:21). Bible✶ study is not finished until we have asked the questions: How is this Word to affect what I am, what I believe, what I do, and how I relate to others? How is it to influence my whole life?

As we study the Bible, God's voice breaks in. With humble heart and open mind we listen. What we hear may offend us or convict us or enlighten us. By the Holy Spirit's power it will give us new life and hope. Luther suggested that the Bible student read the Scripture with this prayer for the Holy Spirit on his lips: "Lord, teach me, teach me, teach me."

✶ We may summarize the three steps of a particular Bible study as (1) observation, (2) interpretation, and (3) application.

FOR FURTHER STUDY

Use the three basic questions: What does it say? What does it mean? What does it mean to me? as you study each of the passages below.

Sunday	John 1:14-18
Monday	Matthew 9:35-38
Tuesday	John 15:12-17
Wednesday	Romans 3:19-28
Thursday	Galatians 5:16-24
Friday	Ephesians 2:1-10
Saturday	Psalm 95

References

Bell, Alvin E. *The Gist of the Bible*. Grand Rapids: Zondervan, 1961.
Halley, Henry H. *Bible Handbook*. Chicago: Moody Press. 968 pp.
Holman Study Bible RSV. Philadelphia: A. J. Holman Co., 1962.
Manley, G. T. *The New Bible Handbook*. Chicago: Inter-Varsity, 1949. 465 pp.
See list of other study Bibles, pp. 71 – 73.

Chapter 5

Studying the Bible with Others

Introduction

Practically every Christian family in America has a Bible. In some homes there are several copies. But mere possession is not enough. Too many Bibles lie unused or are "holy ornaments" around the house. We need to be challenged by the remark: "The only Bible you have is the Bible you know!"

Every Bible contains the 66 books received by the Christian church as its canon (rule of faith). These make a printed book of more than 1,300 pages. Yet the question, "How big is your Bible?" is still valid. Actually our personal canon (rule of faith) is that part of the Scriptures we daily operate with as a guide for our lives. We can live only by that part of the Bible we really know.

But more important than this is another question: How well do we know the Christ who comes into our lives through the words of the Scriptures? (John 5:39; 2 Timothy 3:15)

Knowing the Bible doesn't come easy. It requires both reading and study. It comes with personal interest, effort, and a program of study. We can make progress by ourselves if we have the proper tools. But most of us need to set aside time for study. We also need the stimulus of others studying the Bible with us.

The first Christians gathered for worship, study, and discussion to strengthen each other in the apostles' teaching (Acts 2:42), to help a young Christian worker (Acts 18:24-28), to encourage each other for Christian witnessing. Many, we are told, searched the Scriptures daily to make sure their faith had a solid footing (Acts 17:11). When persecution deprived them of the use of the synagogues for their study and worship, they met in homes and formed what some historians call "house churches." In 1 Corinthians 16:19 and Philemon 2 St. Paul speaks of "the church in your house."

Jesus Himself is undoubtedly our best example of teaching through dialog. He knew the value of face-to-face discussion and of questions to arouse thought and clarify issues. Frequently He drove His "students" back into the Scriptures. Recall His conversational teaching of the Emmaus disciples on Easter afternoon (Luke 24:25-35). Again, the discussion between Philip and the Ethiopian in a chariot (Acts 8:31-38) demonstrates our own need for discussion between teacher and student such as we have in the Bible study class.

I. Why Study the Bible in a Class?

1. Let us admit that most of us do not take time to look up the text of a sermon in the Bible and discuss it with the family; in fact, many fail to take time to open their Bibles for family devotions. When we associate ourselves with fellow Christians and set aside a definite period for class study, we begin to put our fingers into the Bible and look at a particular passage of Scripture and examine it more carefully. This greatly increases our time with the Word, assuming that we add one hour of Bible study to the 30-minute sermon to feed our souls and to enrich our lives.

2. The advantages of group study are many. The individual is encouraged to discover for himself, to ask questions, to find solutions. The Bible class provokes discussion, allows time for the give-and-take which Jesus illustrated. Dialog stimulates thinking. A careful analysis of how people learn has proved that discussion groups facilitate better learning.

3. In a study-discussion group all contribute to learning. They share their observations, the meanings they find, and the applications they see. Such self-expression is important. Every person needs such an outlet for his thoughts; otherwise he is overcome with doubts, fears, and erroneous ideas and "bottles up his religion." One educational axiom says: "Impression without expression leads to depression." It is just such discussion that the writer had in mind when he said: "Let us consider how to stir up one another to love and good works, not neglecting to meet together, as is the habit of some, but encouraging one another." (Hebrews 10:24-25)

4. Class discussion usually stimulates a wider, fuller application of Scripture to life, because it brings the thoughts of many minds to bear on a study section, a given situation, or need. Scripture needs to be seen from the wider experience of many persons.

5. We also learn better under a guide who gives us definite assignments, focuses the discussion on a main theme, keeps the purpose before the class, and helps us to become explorers in Scripture. Thus learning becomes more effective in a group than when we are left to our own limited resources in private study.

6. In the Bible study group we usually follow a definite study course, for instance, a single gospel or a survey of the epistles of Paul. We can penetrate more deeply into a single Christian doctrine. We can enter into areas not so well known. Many subjects can be more fully examined in the study group than in the pulpit. Thus the study group is a vital supplement to the sermon. It is essential, if adult Christians are to grow. Mere hearing can never take the place of reading and studying the Scripture.

Thousands of Bible study groups, especially small study groups meeting in homes, are being used all over the Christian world with increasing satisfaction. A study group stimulates confrontation with God, with our fellowmen, and with ourselves.

Some Examples

One group studying the Gospel of John was asked to give a title to each chapter. At the close of the course it had a total view of this gospel. Individual students looked for particular emphases, for instance, the many references to the deity or Godship of Jesus Christ. This doctrine is expressly stated, alluded to, and implied many times. The result was that members of the class were deepened in their conviction of the deity of our Lord. No half dozen isolated passages could have accomplished this. Every book has similar rewards which it will give to the deliberate student. Once he has made such a close study of a book, it becomes his working capital the rest of his life.

A group of young people were studying the Gospel of Mark. They took time to consider Peter's words, "Lo, we have left everything and followed You" (10:28), and the reply of Jesus that no one follows Him without receiving some very large benefits

(vv. 29-30). The discussion turned upon the question: What does Jesus mean to you, in your life in today's world? Out of the hour-long discussion came six great words to help this group understand "what Christ can mean to us." The outcome was: Christ gives us

Peace	Character
Hope	Wisdom
Fellowship	Purpose

Of course, each one of these words was defined in life-situation terms and applied. Every person in the class was confronted with the question: What do I personally and really believe about Jesus Christ? None of us can escape that question. This study hour was so fruitful that I shall never forget it.

II. Many Methods

Just as there are many types of books in Scripture (compare the Psalms with a gospel), so a study method needs to be chosen according to content and the goal of the class. Some books can be studied by chapters. John's Gospel is one of these. It is well "chapterized." Most books are approached best after we see the major themes and divisions, as indicated in the diagrams of Luke and Acts.

Nor need every student begin with the Biblical text. A group may begin with a problem or work project and then ask: How does Scripture speak to this kind of a situation? The practical experience of the Christians in the group is a further resource.

The subject matter sometimes decides the method. When the class is dealing with an area in which it is totally uninformed, the lecture method is needed. The presentation should be followed by questions that clarify the points made or help fill in gaps.

There are strengths and weaknesses in most teaching-learning methods. Thus verse-by-verse study may cut us off from the larger meaning of the paragraph; the lecture approach may become another sermon; the question-and-answer method may result in mere catechizing; and the discussion method may simply become an airing of opinions instead of getting the message of the text.

The type of study course may dictate the most practical method. A survey course demands background reading of whole books.

A doctrinal study suggests examining the passages where a doctrine is most clearly taught. Christian life subjects can be most fruitful when personal experiences and Biblical insights are shared. A skill course (praying or witnessing) is best approached by getting practice — by doing — and then by sharing what we learned in the doing.

The best results are achieved when everyone in the group becomes a participant, looking up pertinent passages, asking questions, drawing conclusions, making applications, and facing each lesson as a "disciple" — not one who has fully learned but who is always learning. The participant's purpose is to be better equipped for his mission in life as a spokesman for Christ. Any method that makes the student free to discover truths for himself is preferable to procedures where all the answers are suggested by the leader.

III. The Vaesteras Method — An Example

During World War II some Christian youths of Sweden developed a group Bible study procedure which has since made its way around the world. It is called the Vaesteras method, after the town where it was first used. The steps are simple. The group selects the passage to be studied. This can be two or three paragraphs or a whole chapter. Time is allowed (before or in class) for each participant to read the section in silence, usually a paragraph at a time. The reader with pencil in hand uses three symbols: a question mark, an arrow, a flame (or star), which he places in the margin. The leader gives the following instructions:

1. QUESTIONS   *As you read,* put a "Q" or question mark (?) in the margin next to words or phrases you do not fully understand or about which you would like to ask a question.

2. ARROWS   *When you find a verse or phrase* that gives you a directive or guideline for faith or life, put an arrow in the margin. If it suggests a service to God, use a vertical arrow ($\uparrow$); if it suggests a service or directive to man, use a horizontal arrow ($\rightarrow$).

3. LIGHTS — *When you discover some new meaning* that never occurred to you before (some fresh new understanding), place a flame or star (*) as a signal in the margin.

Time is allowed for careful, deliberative reading and marking. Then the leader starts the discussion by asking for the questions. What didn't you understand? What question occurred to you as you read? The leader asks the group for answers to the questions and may prod with additional questions. The purpose is to help everyone to a clearer understanding and sharper observation of what the Biblical text really says.

When the questions have been dealt with, the leader asks members to share and discuss the arrows, that is, the directives they found for service to God and man. Now the group is beginning to apply Scripture to life. The leader may ask: How can we apply what we have learned in our personal lives? in our families? in our church? in our community?

Finally the leader asks for new insights gained (lights). Often a passage, read many times before, suddenly yields a fuller meaning as you read it this time. In reading Romans 12:1, for instance, this writer was struck by the word "bodies" (it doesn't say "souls"). This gave him new insights and understanding of the totality of the Christian's commitment to Christ. Usually someone in the group has gained such a new insight.

The leader then moves on to the next paragraph, and the same process is followed.

The purpose is to come to grips with the meaning and message of the text through collaboration in the study group. A conversational tone prevails. Talkativeness and airing pet views are discouraged. Everybody is encouraged to make serious contributions. The leader stimulates by providing leading questions and supplying points not found by the group. The leader is not to become "the answer man," and lecturing is not part of the process. When a question becomes too difficult, it is deferred for further study and report at the next session.

Practice

Using the Vaesteras method described above, discover and

discuss "questions," "arrows," "lights" in one or more of the following passages:

2 Corinthians 5:16-21
Ephesians 4:7-16
Matthew 16:13-20
Romans 12:3-8
1 Peter 2:1-10

The small neighborhood study group holds great promise for effective group Bible study. It has the warmth, depth, and closeness of the early church (Acts 2:42). It develops participation on the part of every person (not achieved in the large class) and develops many leaders (by experience). Equally important is its outreach potential. It is easier to invite neighbors and friends to informal study group meetings in a home at a convenient time during the week than getting them into a church class. Neighborhood small study cells help "the gathered church" become "the scattered church." Each group is encouraged to add an empty chair in the circle as a missionary challenge. When a neighbor or friend is brought to fill it, another empty chair is placed in the circle as a silent reminder of the missionary character of Christ's church.

"I am prepared to predict," says J. Bruce Weaver, "that if the small group idea spreads so that the majority of our members experience it, they'll discover that bearing witness at work, at home, or at play is just as important and just as much 'church work' as serving on the church council or teaching a church school class. They'll also find that the problem of the inactive members will be considerably reduced." *(The Lutheran)*

IV. Spiritually Productive Bible Study

To encourage you to study the Bible, Paul M. Bretscher suggests 10 criteria answering the question: What is spiritually productive Bible study?

1. It is study which looks to the Holy Spirit for guidance and illumination.
2. It is study which leads *into* the Word and not away from it.
3. It is study which never fails to stress the forgiving love of God in Christ.

4. It is study which submits to the Word of Scripture as the truth.
5. It is study which compels the reader to hear God speaking to him personally from the sacred pages.
6. It is study which makes the reader marvel at the wonders of God's revelation in Scripture.
7. It is study which strengthens faith, increases love, and nourishes Christian hope.
8. It is study which results in a profounder understanding of the purposes of life and of the world.
9. It is study which helps the individual to relate himself on God's terms to others: to his family, to the community, to the country, to the world.
10. It is study which stimulates the questions but which also results in Scripture-grounded answers.

FOR FURTHER STUDY

Many different kinds of Bible study guides are available for use in private study or group study. Your church supplies a wide choice. Here is a sample lesson from Oletta Wald's guide for the study of Colossians, *So Live in Him.* It leads the student into Colossians 3:1-17. Use it this week, and report ways in which it helped you. You may wish to engage another member of your family and make it "group" Bible study. This is how the lesson is structured in the Colossians study guide:

THE NEW LIFE IN CHRIST: COLOSSIANS 3:1-17

DIGGING IN—for the Facts: What does the text say?

I. Put Away the Old Life

Colossians 3:1-4. Here we have Paul's summary of what it means to live in Christ. In essence Paul is saying . . .

BECAUSE—you have been raised with Christ (to a new life)
—you have died with Christ (to the old life)
—your life is hid with Christ in God (your security)
—you are to appear with Christ when He returns (your hope)

THEREFORE . . . LIVE ACCORDINGLY!

Now let us consider the *therefore*.

Colossians 3:5-11

When Paul wrote about the old and the new natures, he had much advice to give. First he attacks what does not belong in the Christian life. Note the key admonitions. Underline them in your Bible. List what the Colossians were admonished to do and the reasons given.

A. PUT TO DEATH—the sins of passion and desire. Which ones? (3:5) _____

Why? (3:6-7) _____

_____

B. PUT AWAY—the sins of disposition and speech. Which ones? (3:8-9) _____

Why? (3:9-10) _____

C. What is the relationship of 3:11 to the previous verses and to those which follow? _____

II. *Put on the New Life*

Study Colossians 3:12-17

The Christian is not just to put away the sinful desires, habits, and actions of the past life, but he is to manifest the graces and virtues which have their source in the new nature. The new life is to develop more and more into the likeness of Christ. The old nature and the new nature are always at odds with each other, struggling for supremacy. We choose which is to dominate us by setting our minds, either on the ways of the old life or the new life.

Again note the key admonitions in this section and the reason for their significance. Underline the key words in your Bible. Summarize the admonitions in your own words.

A. PUT ON (3:12) _____

Also (3:13) _____

Why? _____

B. PUT ON (3:14) _____ Why? _____

C. LET (3:15) _____

Why? _____

D. LET (3:16) _____

How and When? _____

  E. DO (3:17) _____

DIGGING DEEPER — for Understanding

III. *What Does Paul Mean?*

While Paul was writing to persons who lived some 2,000 years ago, his advice is equally challenging to us today. For gaining deeper insight into the meanings of words and phrases you will find the dictionary very helpful, especially in the study of attitudes and actions Christians are to PUT OFF and PUT ON. Consider some of the following questions:

A. Think about the key phrase in the passage: PUT TO DEATH, PUT AWAY, PUT ON, LET RULE, LET DWELL. What is involved as to feelings, will, and actions if a person is to follow each of these admonitions? Why do you think Paul used each of these key admonitions in the way he did?

B. Try matching some of the vices that are to be *put to death* and to be *put away* with some of the virtues that are to be *put on*. In what way will one crowd out the other? What does this tell us about living the Christian life?

C. Is it possible for a non-Christian as well as a Christian to follow these admonitions? What will make the difference? What is the work of the Holy Spirit as we seek to *put off* and *put on?* What is the place of prayer?

D. Which of Paul's admonitions have something to say about our relationship with other church members? with other races? with the members of our personal families?

GROWING IN CHRIST

IV. *What Is Paul Saying to Us?*

Growth in Christ is not like climbing a ladder so that "day by day we get better and better." Rather it is more like a plant growing, gradually embedding its roots more deeply into the soil, producing new branches, blossoms, and fruit. Change comes from within, but reveals itself in outward manifestations.

The key to growth in Christ is found in Colossians 3:16.

A. *Meditate on Colossians 3:16 and memorize it.*

1. Note WHAT we are to do—Let the Word of Christ DWELL *in you* RICHLY. . . . Think of the starvation diet most of us live on!

What are some of the things you should be doing if the Word of Christ is to dwell in you richly? _____

2. Note the WHEN—*as you teach and admonish one another in all wisdom.* . . . Think of your own Bible study group, sitting in a circle, teaching and encouraging one another, as you share the wisdom you have gained through personal study and experiences. What can you do to help the members in your study group grow in their Christian faith? Name three things _____

_____

3. Note the HOW—*with thankfulness in your hearts to God.* . . . Note the number of times Paul emphasizes the importance of thanksgiving in relation to other admonitions. IF we permit Christ's Word to dwell in our hearts richly, IF we permit Christ's peace to rule our hearts, IF WE SHARE and encourage each other in study and prayer, how should these experiences fill us with joy and thankfulness? _____

How do they enable us to *put off* the old nature and *put on* the new?

_____

B. *Apply Paul's admonitions to daily life.*

To PUT ON means to deliberately do something, not because we feel like doing it but because we are one of God's chosen ones. How would you apply Paul's admonitions in the following situations?

1. When you are working or living with someone who is disagreeable.
2. When factions begin to develop in a church.
3. When you feel bitter about the way someone has treated you.
4. When someone disagrees with your interpretation of some doctrine.
5. When some lonely person reaches out for your friendship.
6. When you view some of the literature and movies of today.

References

Coiner, Harry G. *Teaching the Word to Adults.* St. Louis: Concordia Publishing House, 1962. 129 pp.

Feucht, O. E. *Bible Study in the Life of the Church.* St. Louis: Board of Parish Education (reprint).

_____. *Small Bible Study Groups.* St. Louis: Concordia Publishing House, 1961. 13 pp.

Wald, Oletta. *The Joy of Discovery.* Minneapolis: Banner Press, 1956. 92 pp.

Chapter 6

Getting the Message of a Whole Book

Each book of the Bible is a separate unit. It has its own author and style, its own history and background, and its own specific purpose and message. If we are to understand the Bible, we must first understand the Bible "bookwise," that is, we must understand each book by itself and then see its relation to other books of the Scriptures and to the Bible's unique message of salvation in Christ.

This means getting a grasp of the entire book. It's something like reading *Uncle Tom's Cabin.* You don't get the story unless you read the entire book. To see less than the whole Biblical book is to see less than God gave us. This approach develops balance and gives us an overview. It keeps us from overemphasizing or underemphasizing certain parts of Scripture. It permits the proper attention to context. It leads us directly into the book itself, its chapters, paragraphs, verses, and words.

Martin Luther compared Bible reading to picking fruit. First you pick up the ripened fruit that has fallen to the ground (book as a whole). Then you shake the limbs (chapters). Next you climb into the branches to find more fruit (paragraphs). Finally you reach out to smaller twigs and look behind leaves to get some luscious cherry or peach (verses and words).

We have already noted (Chapter 4, see diagram) the larger divisions of the Gospel According to St. Luke and the Acts of the Apostles, and have seen how closely these books are related to each other. Most books have a structure or form. We might say we can divide them into so many rooms of one house, each room a little different; but when they are put together, they form one building.

However, not all books of the Bible are unified, that is, so structured that they fall into major, logical parts. Some books are collections of sayings, like books of quotations. We call them *nonunified books*. The Proverbs of Solomon is such a book. The first nine chapters, addressed to "My son," are followed by a miscellaneous collection of 374 proverbs. Ecclesiastes, also called the Preacher, is likewise proverbial in character. The Psalms can be grouped in five major divisions and are comparable to a book of poems. In these books each verse may be a unit for thought and devotion.

Not all the books need the same kind of study. The main message of some can be gained by a cursory reading. Many books however call for careful study, notably the gospels and letters of the New Testament. These books, as well as their individual chapters, paragraphs, and verses, are highly relevant when applied to the modern scene and Christian living in our time. But we must see the entire message before we look at the details. How do we get the message of a total book? We will learn how by taking an overview of the Epistle to the Ephesians. One of its main themes is "The Church." We shall look at the whole letter from that point of view.

The Book of Ephesians: The Church and Its Mission

Introduction

Before studying a book we need to know the author, visualize the intended audience, and get its historical background. Find the city of Ephesus in Asia Minor on one of the maps in your Bible. Perhaps your Bible has a map showing St. Paul's three missionary journeys. After locating Ephesus, read Acts 20:13-38 for background. Notice the fine relationship between Paul and the Christians at Ephesus.

Returning to Jerusalem on his third missionary journey, the apostle stopped at Miletus in Asia Minor to meet the elders of the church at Ephesus. He counseled them to feed the church of God faithfully. At Jerusalem Paul was arrested for preaching the Gospel and was eventually imprisoned in Rome. Many scholars believe it was during this Roman imprisonment that he wrote Philippians, Colossians, Philemon, and Ephesians. The apparent date of Ephesians is A. D. 63.

Ephesus was one of the three great commercial centers of the eastern Mediterranean world, also a great political and religious center. There stood the temple of Diana, considered one of the Seven Wonders of the world. It was 425 feet long and 239 feet wide. Its roof rested on 100 columns, each 55 feet high. The temple was built over a period of 220 years. Here at Ephesus was also the great amphitheater on the side of Mount Coressus, seating 24,500. Like many other cities, Ephesus was the focus of idolatry, superstition, wealth, luxury, and vice.

The Letter to the Ephesians reveals the splendors of God's grace in our eternal election, redemption, conversion, and sanctification. Because of its loftiness and the recurrence of the "heavenly places" phrase (five times), it has been called the "epistle of the ascension." It contains the New Testament charter of Christian education. Look for its emphasis on Christian growth in chapters 1 and 3–6. It gives us our noblest conception of marriage and Christian family life. Above all, Ephesians is a book about the church described as the *body of Christ*. The companion volume, Colossians, shows Christ as the glorified *Head* of this body.

The book has a vertical thrust (man's relation to God) in its doctrinal section (chapters 1–3), and a horizontal thrust (man's relation to man) in the practical section (chapters 4–6). Christian doctrine, Christian experience, and Christian ethics are inseparably united.

We first note *the salutation*—1:1-2. How does it compare with letters written today and with the letterheads which we use? We are going to look at this letter under its specific theme "The Church and Its Mission." The Bible gives no specific titles for its books. How do we find the chief message—the message that distinguishes one book from another? We find the key to this letter in Ephesians 1:9-10:

> He has made known to us in all wisdom and insight the mystery of His will, according to His purpose which He set forth in Christ as a plan for the fullness of time, to unite all things in Him, things in heaven and things on earth.

We shall look at five major aspects of the book. Please note that we are using thought divisions, not chapter divisions, in this analysis of the book. Put your findings in a notebook.

I. God's Wonderful Plan for You, 1:3-23

We take "plan" from the key verses, 9-10. Begin with vv. 3-14. Note the sweep of this section with regard to time (from eternity to eternity) and with regard to the universal reign of Christ. But how shall we break it into units? This section can be seen as a "hymn" with three stanzas. Read them as such: first stanza, 3 to 6a; second stanza, 6b to 12; third stanza, 13 and 14. Now note that it is a hymn of praise, with the words "praise" and "glory" in each refrain: vv. 6a, 12, and 14. Read the section again and note that it praises God the Father, God the Son, and God the Holy Spirit. Now look at each stanza separately.

Read vv. 3-6a. As you read, find the answers to these questions: Who acts? What does He do? When did it take place? Where? How? Why? These questions are very helpful in almost all Bible study. How is God the Father related to the plan?

Proceed to the second stanza, vv. 6b-12. How is God the Son, Jesus Christ, related to the plan? By what special name is He called? Now find answers to the questions: Who? What is the secret of God's great plan? What did the Son provide? When did it happen? Where? How? Why?

You are now ready for the third stanza, vv. 13-14. What is the new element here? Who is introduced? What is His function? Why is the Holy Spirit necessary to carry out God's eternal plan? Find the answers to your questions: Who? What? When? Where? How? Why? What light does Romans 8:16 throw on these verses?

The first chapter of Ephesians is not the simplest, and yet it is one of the most rewarding in the New Testament. Reread it to notice how often the "in Christ" phrase or its equivalent appears. Underscore each reference to Christ. How many times do you find such a reference? You might summarize vv. 3-14 with the phrase, "All in Christ — all by grace." Why? The TEV makes it plain.

Read vv. 15-20a and note the content and purpose of Paul's prayer for the Ephesian Christians. What power can all Christians draw on? What personal goal does this suggest for your own growth in discipleship? (Vv. 16-19)

Vv. 20b-23 deal with the reign of the ascended Christ and give us a description of the church as His working body on earth. In what sense is Christ (the Head) completed and fulfilled in His members (the body)? Look for additional images of the church in the rest of this letter.

II. The Gospel Transforms Us, Unites Us, and Equips the Church for Mission, 2:1—3:13

This larger portion breaks down into a number of sections.

2:1-10 — Conversion is the evidence of God's power in the church. It answers the question: How do we become members of Christ's body? Why is conversion necessary? How is it like a spiritual resurrection? In what sense is it completely a gift? Why are vv. 8-9 significant doctrinally? How are they related to chapter 1? How does v. 10 indicate the purpose of our rebirth? What does this section mean for you personally?

2:11-18 — Shows that being redeemed by the blood of Christ and embodied in Christ's body (the church) erases the barriers between Jew and Gentile. Why did prejudices exist between Jews and Gentiles? Note the points of separation (v. 12). What is the wall that Christ abolished? (vv. 13-18). How did Jesus "make peace"? What is meant by "one new man"? How does reconciliation to God help us to be reconciled with people? (V. 18)

2:19-22 — Gives us a number of additional images of the church. What are the images, symbols, or pictures employed to give us a better understanding of it? In what sense is the Holy Spirit the Architect and we the builders of Christ's church on earth?

What comparisons does Paul use to describe the church?

Ephesians 1:22-23 _____

2:19 _____

2:20 _____

2:21-22 _____

3:1-13 — The mission of the apostle and of the church today is described here. Note that Paul considers his ministry as his greatest stewardship. What is the "mystery" that Paul is unveiling at this point? (vv. 7-13). Why does he count his mission a great privilege? Why does only the Gospel give access to God? What is our part in this mission? (Enter your findings in a notebook.)

III. How God Prepares Us for Our Mission, 3:14—4:16

The apostle begins this section with a prayer for the spiritual growth of the Ephesian Christians (3:14-21). What goals does he suggest for them? By whose power can they attain these goals?

In 4:1-6 he speaks about the harmony and unity in Christ's church, listing *seven* points of unity which the Holy Spirit produces, vv. 4-6 (list in your notebook), and *four* points which call upon the Christian to express this unity and harmony, vv. 1-3 (list in notebook). Who creates the unity of the church? Who helps to preserve it?

Beginning with v. 7 the apostle describes how Christ's members then and today are to be trained for their mission. To whom did the ascending Lord supply gifts? (4:7-10). Vv. 11-16 indicate that we have pastors and teachers to equip us (God's people) for our mission wherever we live and work in the world. What does it say to you about your purpose in life as a Christian? How is the purpose to be achieved in the fellowship of the Christian congregation? How are members of a congregation to serve one another? What is the role of the laity in carrying out God's mission today?

IV. The Witness of the Church in Our Lives, 4:17—5:20

The apostle now develops four contrasts to point out the difference the Gospel makes in a believer's life. There are four ways in which the Christian "walks worthy of the Lord" and expresses his Christian vocation, 4:1. God calls us not merely to separated living but to distinctively Christian living.

Read 4:17-24. What is the contrast? Give it a subtitle.

Read 4:25-5:2. What is this contrast? Give it a subtitle.

Read 5:3-14. What contrast is shown here? Give it your own subtitle. _____

Read 5:15-20. What contrast is to be found here? Give it your own subtitle. _____

Note the emphasis on the Christian's Witness: by what he *says* and by how he *lives*.

V. Living and Conquering in the Lord
(Our mission in four human relationships), 5:21-6:20

The apostle in these verses appeals to Christians to live out their mission in all earthly relationships. The basic principle is found in 5:21. How is living in the Lord to be shown?

In the marriage relationship? 5:22-33 _____

_____

In the parent-child relationship? 6:1-4 _____

_____

In the master-slave, employer-employee relationship? 6:5-9 ___

_____

After giving these examples, the apostle calls for a militant faith, 6:10-17. As you read it, identify the enemy and list the Christian's weapons. Note that the sword of the Spirit is the Word of God, the Gospel.

The enemy: Who is he? _____

           What are his traits? _____

The Christian: Who supplies his strength? _____

           What is he to be? to do? _____

           What are his weapons (the armor)?

           v. 14 _____ _____

           v. 15 _____ v. 16 _____

           v. 17 _____ _____

The mission of the Christian and of the church is a formidable one. We are likely to ask: Where can we get the strength? Vv. 18-20 tell us that we are never alone, that Christ is our unseen Commander.

The Epilogue, 6:21-24. The letter closes with a call to Christian brotherhood. What do these closing words mean to you?

This book of the New Testament is a call to walk worthily (ch. 4), live distinctively (ch. 5), and stand courageously (ch. 6).

Through the centuries this letter has been translated into more than 1,000 languages and sent out into all the world. It has now come to you. And through you it is to reach others. Before laying the book aside, ask yourself the question: What shall I do with the message God gives me in Ephesians? What can it do to refashion my life? What pattern of life and action does it suggest to my congregation? How can I share its message with my friends?

70

SUPPLEMENT: TOOLS FOR THE BIBLE STUDENT

1. A Good Study Bible

The Chain Reference Bible (KJV text), compiled by Frank Charles Thompson (sold by Kirkbride, Indianapolis, Ind.), is a storehouse of excellent help with book introductions and topical classification of verses.

The Holy Bible, A Reference Edition (KJV text), American Bible Society, 1962. It is well paragraphed with subheads. Poetic sections are shown as poetry. The 338 pages of helps include a concordance, aerial perspective maps in color, lists of alternative readings and renderings, and words that have changed meaning since 1611.

Holman Study Bible (RSV text) contains an introduction to and an outline of each book of the bible. Poetic sections are shown as poetry. Helpful background articles are: Light from the Dead Sea Scrolls, the Bible and Modern Science, the Archaeology of the Bible, Between the Testaments, the Chronology of the Bible. Also included: a 191-page concordance, colored maps, and a helpful foreword. (A. J. Holman Co.)

Concordia Reference Bible (RSV text), 1966. Contains a concordance, a 146-page dictionary, 12 pages of new Bible maps, and a 6-page index. Center references.

2. A Bible Word Book

This is one of the most important tools, since it points out how the various Biblical terms are used in the Old and New Testaments. It shows in what connection and with what variation (depending on context and period of use) the terms occur. Such word books are *A Companion to the Bible,* by J. J. Von Allmen (New York: Oxford University Press, 1958), and Alan Richardson's *A Theological Word Book of the Bible* (Macmillan, 1957 — available in large paperback edition).

3. One or More Modern Translations

The improvements in modern translations vary. Most translations, such as the Revised Standard Version, the New English Bible, the interpretive paraphrases by J. B. Phillips, and the American Bible Society's *Good News for Modern Man* (New Testament paperback by Robert G. Bratcher) give excellent aid to the modern reader. For a brief evaluation of these and other modern translations and their worth to the Bible student, get Robert Bratcher's pamphlet "Why So Many Bibles?" (Concordia Publishing House), or Dewey M. Beegle's book, *God's Word into English* (Wm. B. Eerdmans, 1960).

4. Bible Concordance

A concordance lists passages that contain the same word, enabling the reader to find many references to the same word or subject. Some are so complete as to contain practically every appearance of a certain word in the Old and New Testaments. Abbreviated concordances are found in the better study Bibles. The most complete concordances are: *Analytical Concordance to the Bible* (words of KJV text, but showing the Hebrew and Greek words they translate), by Robert Young (Funk and Wagnalls, 1917), *Nelson's Complete Concordance of the Revised Standard Version Bible* (Thomas Nelson & Sons, 1957).

5. Bible Dictionary

A Bible dictionary gives brief descriptions and additional historical, geographical, and theological material on persons, places, concepts, and doctrines related to the Bible. Condensed Bible dictionaries are found in some study Bibles. Such a small, helpful book (146 pages) is *Concordia Bible Dictionary* by E. L. Lueker, available in paperback (Concordia, 1963). More extensive are: *The New Compact Bible Dictionary*, T. Alton Bryant (Grand Rapids: Zondervan, 1967, 621 pp., 5,000 entries, over 250 pictures); *Westminster Dictionary of the Bible*, J. D. Davis, revised by H. S. Gehman (Philadelphia: Westminster Press, 692 pp., 1944); *Unger's Bible Dictionary*, Merrill F. Unger (Chicago: Moody Press, 1957, 1,200 pp., 7,000 articles, 500 illustrations); *New Bible Dictionary*, J. D. Douglas (Grand Rapids: Eerdmans, 1962, 1,375 pp., 2,300 all *new* articles, 300 drawings). See catalog of Concordia Publishing House for more complete descriptions and prices.

6. Bible Commentary

The commentary is listed last, not because it is insignificant but because there is danger that we go to the commentary too soon. This defeats the making of Bible students. There are many commentaries on the market. Among the newer ones which take into consideration more recent scholarship as well as an evangelical approach to Scripture are: *The Layman's Bible Commentary*, whole Bible in 25 small (4¾×7¼) volumes, ed. B. H. Kelly (Richmond: John Knox Press, 1959–63); *Laymen's Pocket Commentaries*, New Testament only, 17 small (4¼×7¾) volumes, Chas. R. Erdman (Philadelphia: Westminster Press, from 1925 on); *Tyndale New Testament Commentaries*, 30 volumes (5¼×7¼), ed. R. V. G. Tasker (Grand Rapids: Eerdmans, from 1961 on); commentaries on the New Testament with applications: *The Daily Bible Study Series*, 20 volumes (4¼×6½), Wm. Barclay (Philadelphia: Westminster Press, from 1956 on). Or you may prefer a one-volume commentary (always limited in scope, of course), like *The New Bible Commentary*, Davidson, Stibbs, Kevan (Grand Rapids: Eerdmans, 1956), 1,199 pp., 6¼×9½.

FOR FURTHER STUDY

When asked how he became a Bible student, one Christian leader replied, "By reading the whole book of Ephesians every day for two weeks." Can you duplicate his experience? Each reading will give you deeper and new impressions. At the end of *seven* readings you will get a satisfaction and competence you do not have now. You will be able to see more clearly its structure, message, and practical meaning for your life. This is your assignment —

Monday   *Reread Ephesians*, calling to mind what you learned in class.

Tuesday   Read Ephesians 1:1-23. Keep the five-point outline in mind throughout.

Wednesday   Reread the whole book, but give special attention to section 2:1 – 3:13.

Thursday   Read it again, but reflect on the meaning of 3:14 – 4:16 for your own life and your congregation.

| *Friday* | Reread all six chapters, but spend a little more time on 4:17—5:20. |
| *Saturday* | Do your seventh reading, meditating especially on 5:21—6:24. |

References

Blair, Edward P. *The Bible and You.* Nashville: Abingdon, 1953. Chs. 3 and 4.

Hegland, Martin. *Getting Acquainted with the Bible.* Minneapolis: Augsburg, 1944. 239 pp.

Chapter 7

The Nature and Form of the Bible

Introduction

In the preceding six chapters we have discussed the personal use of the Bible and learned how to read and study the Bible profitably, both by ourselves and with others. Then we examined the procedures by which we may get the distinctive message of a particular book (Ephesians). If for us the Bible is to be a book to live by, we need first to acquire the skills for rewarding Bible use.

In the following chapters we shall take up some of the questions which everyone approaching the Bible asks: How did the Bible come to us? What is meant by inspiration? Why do we call it the Word of God? What gives to it its authority and power? What are the basic principles for sound Bible interpretation? We shall try to get an aeroplane view of Scripture and see the relationship between the Old Covenant and the New.

To understand the Bible, we must know its nature and form. This is all the more important if we are to deal factually with some of the diverse views of the Bible held today. This chapter challenges us to learn more about the human and the divine aspects of the Scripture, about revelation and Scripture, about the way the Bible itself uses the term "Word of God." We will learn how the books of the Old and New Testaments were collected and about the early manuscripts and translations.

I. The Nature and Purpose of the Scriptures

✳   The Holy Scriptures are the record of God's mighty acts and their interpretation by prophets and apostles inspired by God.

✳   The Bible is both a revelation and a record. Revelation means the making known of something that would have remained hidden if God had not proclaimed it in some manner. God has many ways of making Himself known. "The heavens declare the glory of God" (Psalm 19:1). From the creation of the world God's invisible nature, His eternal power and deity, are perceived in the things which He made. (Romans 1:19-20)

God used visions and dreams to reveal His will on particular occasions (Genesis 15:1; Daniel 2:19; Matthew 2:19). However, what has been revealed would have been lost to us had God not recorded this revelation through prophets and apostles (Ephesians 3:1-7; Deuteronomy 29:29). Both in His acts and in His Word, recorded for us in Scripture, God reveals Himself to us even today.

While nature does reveal God, no tree, flower, or constellation of stars can tell us the special message of God's mercy and love in Jesus Christ. For this we needed God's special revelation.

The Bible is unique among all books. It explains our place in the universe. It tells us we are not alone in an unfriendly world. It tells us who we really are and gives us a purpose in life. Here are the answers to the searching questions which every man at one time or another asks. And here we have God's answers. In this sense the Bible is a book that will always appeal to man because every human being asks these questions. The Bible is also significant because apart from it much of the history and literature of the Western world cannot be fully understood.

From it we learn that God has long been seeking to enter into fellowship with us and wishes to give us life abundant here and hereafter. It is God's self-revelation of His love and mercy. The Word of God's grace bestows the unique gift of faith through its regenerating power. The Letter to the Hebrews gives us a good introduction to the book:

> In many and various ways God spoke of old to our fathers by the prophets; but in these last days He has spoken to us by a Son, whom He appointed the heir of all things, through whom also He created the world. *Hebrews 1:1-2*

Our salvation rests upon the life, suffering, death, and resurrection of our Lord Jesus Christ. This salvation was revealed in the events and prophetic messages of the Old Testament. It is interpreted as the greatest act of God, both in prophecy and in the fulfillment recorded in the New Testament. To preserve this message for us, God gave us a gift, the Scripture. The church is responsible to God for the use and distribution of this gift.

II. The Bible and Inspiration

The Bible is a very human book. It went through the processes of development very much like any other book. The writers recorded the messages, history, customs, beliefs, philosophies, trials, problems and errors, fears and hopes of the people of many generations. No book searches the chambers of the human heart so thoroughly and relentlessly as does the Bible. No book reveals the fears, animosities, joys, and passions of its writers so clearly and movingly. If you would learn to know man as he really is, as he thinks, feels, and desires, and what he is like when stripped of all pretense, read the Bible. We sometimes forget that the Bible is a human book. It has to be that in order to speak to human beings. In this sense the Bible is dipped right out of life.

At the same time the Bible by its own testimony is a divine book. It is referred to and treated as the Word of God. Jesus expounded it in the Capernaum synagogue and in many other places. His references to the Old Testament are recorded in each of the gospels. He said: "Think not that I have come to abolish the Law and the Prophets [that is, Scripture]; I have come not to abolish them but to fulfill them. For truly, I say to you, till heaven and earth pass away, not an iota, not a dot, will pass from the Law until all is accomplished" (Matthew 5:17-18). The same is true of the apostles. In the Book of Acts Stephen, Peter, and Paul are constantly referring to the Old Testament as being fulfilled in Christ. (Acts 2; 7; 13)

Thus we see the Bible has a very human aspect and a divine aspect. We should not by rationalizing explain away either the divine factor or the human factor in God's plan to give us the Old and the New Testament. God used ordinary men to write because He wanted to reach ordinary men.

The prophets and apostles were more than mere recorders. Their writing was more than an independent, human activity.

Frequently they wrote what was beyond their own knowledge and experience or even comprehension.

> The prophets who prophesied of the grace that was to be yours searched and inquired about this salvation; they inquired what person or time was indicated by the Spirit of Christ within them when predicting the sufferings of Christ and the subsequent glory. It was revealed to them that they were serving not themselves but you, in the things which have now been announced to you by those who preached the good news to you through the Holy Spirit sent from heaven, things into which angels long to look.
> *1 Peter 1:10-12*

Speaking of the apostles' writing, Peter refers to two facts: the apostles were eyewitnesses, and the Holy Spirit moved the writers.

> For we did not follow cleverly devised myths when we made known to you the power and coming of our Lord Jesus Christ, but we were eyewitnesses of His majesty. . . . First of all you must understand this, that no prophecy of Scripture is a matter of one's own interpretation, because no prophecy ever came by the impulse of man, but men moved by the Holy Spirit spoke from God.
> *2 Peter 1:16, 20*

The apostle Paul simply says: "All Scripture is inspired by God" (2 Timothy 3:16). We call this inspiration. The writers were instruments of God. They were His spokesmen. Yet they did not lay aside their own background, training, and ways of expressing themselves. And they wrote out of the human situation in which they found themselves. They recorded history as God made it. But they did more. They *interpreted* it as God would have it understood.

Various theories have been propounded with regard to the inspiration of the Scripture. Some are very mechanistic. They rule out the human side of the Bible's composition. In some instances the exact words were given and written down as direct quotations from God (Exodus 24:3-4). We have evidence in Scriptures that the writers used extant sources. The Holy Spirit so guided the writers that they selected what He wished to use.

While we do not know the precise manner of inspiration, we do know that the Bible is inspired. It is a word of power and authority. It gives us the vivifying, life-giving Word because it brings to us the Giver of life, Jesus Christ. (John 6:63)

III. The Word of God and Scriptures

The terms "Word" and "Scripture" are not always used coextensively in the Bible. Word may mean the oral Word, the spoken message before it was written. It can mean the recorded Word. It can mean the Gospel of Jesus Christ. We must distinguish how the Bible in a particular place (according to context) is using the term. Word did not mean the Bible before there was an Old or a New Testament.

In a few instances the Bible also uses the term Word (*Logos* in the Greek) when it refers to Jesus Christ. It does so in John 1:1, 14; 1 John 1:1; Revelation 19:13. Christ is the living Word of whom the written Word speaks and whom it declares and reveals to us. Therefore we speak of Christ as the incarnate Word, the Word made flesh.

Word sometimes means the creative word which God spoke and by which the earth and the heavens were made. (Genesis 1:1, 3, 6, 9; Psalm 33:6; Hebrews 11:3)

Frequently the term Word (Word of God) is employed to designate the message of God's promise and grace, which in the New Testament is called the Gospel (Isaiah 55:10-11; Acts 8:4-5; Ephesians 1:13; Colossians 1:5). In Acts 20:32 it's called "the Word of His Grace." The words of Jesus are life-giving words (John 5:24; 6:63; 1 Peter 1:23-25). When the Gospel (Word) "increased" through preaching, disciples "multiplied."

> The Word of God increased; and the number of the disciples multiplied greatly in Jerusalem, and a great many of the priests were obedient to the faith.　　*Acts 6:7*

But the term Word of God is also used of the written words of the Scripture. The Bible, as a book of inspired writings, is the vehicle by which God still reveals His Word, both Law and Gospel, to man. So then both the *spoken* words of Jesus and of the prophets and apostles and the *written* words recorded by the latter at God's direction are definitely called the Word of God (1 Peter 1:10-12; 2 Peter 1:19-21). In fact, God's Spirit caused men of God to write down what God said (Jeremiah 30:1-4; 36:2). The prophets state again and again that their message was given to them by God (Jeremiah 1:2; Hosea 1:1; Joel 1:1). When King Josiah found the neglected books of the Law, he called them the Word of the Lord. (2 Chronicles 34:21)

There are other religious "scriptures" in the world that offer intellectually attractive ideas, or cultivate mystical escape from life's problems, or provide moral precepts for training in self-discipline and human achievement. But none of them offer the gift of God's grace in Christ as do the Scriptures.

Because the Spirit comes to us through the words of Scripture, the Bible is what no other book is: a word of power making us wise unto salvation through faith in Christ Jesus (2 Timothy 3:15-17).

> The Word of God is living and active, sharper than any two-edged sword, piercing to the division of the soul and spirit, of joints and marrow, and discerning the thoughts and intentions of the heart. *Hebrews 4:12*

IV. The Authority of Scripture

Jesus' own use of the Old Testament shows that it was the source and norm of faith for the Israelite believer. To a questioner He said: "What is written in the Law? How do you read?" To the Pharisees He said: "The Scripture cannot be broken" (John 10:35). The apostles not only quoted Old Testament passages but also referred authoritatively to their own (New Testament) writings. (2 Peter 3:15; Ephesians 3:3-5; 1 Corinthians 2:1, 10, 12)

Religion becomes human, speculative philosophy when it lacks authentic revelation, such as we have in the Scriptures. The church has no place to stand once it divorces itself from the Scriptures. Then it is subject to its own self-deceptions. That is why all Christendom in the last analysis looks to the Bible for its teaching.

The Scripture is the source and standard of Christian doctrine. Martin Luther insisted that Scripture take precedence over all human opinions, including his own and those of the church fathers. The Formula of Concord, one of the Lutheran Confessions makes it clear that a Lutheran is an evangelical Christian who tests the validity of his teaching by asking: Is it based on the Bible?

Holy Scripture remains the only judge, rule, and norm according to which as the only touchstone all doctrines should and must be understood and judged as good or evil, right or wrong.

Other symbols and other writings are not judges like Holy Scripture, but merely witnesses and expositions of the faith, setting forth how at various times the Holy Scriptures were understood in the church of God by contemporaries with reference to controverted articles, and how contrary teachings were rejected and condemned. (*The Book of Concord*, Theodore G. Tappert, editor. Muhlenberg Press, 1959. P. 465)

V. The Form of the Bible

The Bible is a varied library of many books. Each book has its own date and setting and speaks to a specific set of problems and circumstances. The books of the Bible were written by men who lived in a number of cultures quite different from our Western civilization. For instance, Psalm 137 was written during the time when God's people were exiled in Babylon. Most scholars believe the books of the Bible were written over a period of 1,500 years, from approximately 1400 B. C. to A. D. 100.

Each book appeared separately and existed for some time before it was included by the people of God in the canon. In our Bible the books are arranged not in the order of their appearance (chronologically) but according to content and literary type, much as one arranges the books in his own library today. The arrangement in various editions of the Hebrew Scriptures was not always the same.

The individual books also vary greatly. Some are systematically organized around a single general theme. For example, the four gospels tell us of the ministry and mission of our Lord. Some books cover a span of history. Some contain the sermons of a prophet. The New Testament letters are directed either to congregations or to individuals and their particular needs. Other books of the Bible do not have a central theme. They are more like collections of poems and prayers, for instance, the Psalms and the Book of Proverbs.

The Bible bears the imprint of many people, statesmen, a herdsman, soldiers, fishermen, and a physician. It reports the work of kings, priests, scribes, prophets, and apostles. It contains the visions of Isaiah, Ezekiel, Daniel, and John. In it we find simple prose and Hebrew poetry. Its narratives of men and women give us many examples of human sinfulness and frailty, of rebellion, murder, rape, trickery, and war. The sins of men and women have been recorded in the Bible for our warning. (1 Corinthians 10:11)

The Bible is not (as some suppose) an arranged summary of doctrines. It was not written like a catechism that gives precise theological answers. Instead it is a historical book. It shows God breaking into history through men and events, which history He guides and controls in keeping with His redemptive purpose. Though historical, it is a book in which God makes known, by recorded word and deed, His eternal plan for man's salvation.

Nor is the Bible just a compilation of many types of literature. It has unity in its diversity. That unity is given by the Holy Spirit. Christ Himself, to whom both prophecy and fulfillment bear witness, is the unifying Person.

Though the Bible is a very old book, it is immensely relevant for our day. The modern reader of any land or language finds in it the story of himself and the answer to his deepest needs.

VI. The Canonical Scriptures

The Bible is not an accident. At various times and places over the centuries God directed not only the writing but also guided the gathering and editing of what we call now the Old and New Testament canon.

The word "canon" means a measuring line or rule, a critical standard by which something is judged. Used of the Bible, it means a list of those books which were received by the people of God as authentic and possessing authority.

The Old Testament records the fact that the Pentateuch (first five books) formed a unit and was preserved and read to the people. At later times the historical books, the prophetical books, and the "Writings," which included Psalms and Proverbs, were collected.

Jesus alludes to a threefold organization of the Old Testament in Luke 24:44 (the Law of Moses, the Prophets, the Psalms).

It is commonly thought that several centuries before Christ Ezra and perhaps other leaders formed the canon by gathering the scrolls that were accepted as the authoritative Old Testament Scriptures.

Similarly, already by the beginning of the second century of our era the first letters and gospels of the New Testament were received by the churches as given by the Spirit. An early listing of "accepted books" dates back to the last quarter of the second century, and a final listing of the New Testament books as we have them today is recorded in the Easter letter of Athanasius in A. D. 367.

From 2 Peter 3:16 we can assume that the gospels and letters were circulated soon after they were written. William Barclay writes in his *The Making of the Bible:* "It is clear that by A. D. 100 Paul's letters had been collected and were widely known and widely accepted."

It must be remembered that the individual writings of the Old Testament were accepted as the Word of God at the time of writing (Joshua 1:7-8; 11:15; Judges 3:4; 1 Kings 2:3; 2 Kings 14:6; 2 Chronicles 23:18). This is true also of the New Testament books (Ephesians 3:3-5; 2 Peter 3:15-16). For a fuller treatment see F. F. Bruce, *The Books and the Parchments* (1963 edition), Chapter VIII and Appendices I and II.

It is interesting to note that the canon was not established by some official church convention but evidently by consensus of the churches after years of use. "The New Testament and the young Christian church grew up together" is the way one scholar puts it. "A book first has divine authority based on its inspiration, and then attains canonicity due to its general acceptance as a divine product. No church council by its decrees can make the books of the Bible authoritative. The books of the Bible possess their own authority and indeed had this authority long before there were any councils of the church. . . . The church does not control the canon but the canon controls the church." (Neil R. Lightfoot, *How We Got the Bible,* pp. 82, 87)

"But what about the Apocrypha?" you ask. That word means "hidden or concealed." It was used when referring to 15 books written in the intertestamental period. The books were not considered canonical but as "wholesome reading." First Maccabees and the Wisdom of Sirach are especially helpful. There are also some New Testament-related apocryphal books, like the Gospel According to St. Thomas (114 verses) and the Acts of Paul. But they are spurious and fanciful and do not belong in the canon.

The rules of the canon are not specifically known to us. They certainly included apostolicity, marks of inspiration, recognition by the people of God, and clear testimony to Jesus Christ.

We must not forget that the church of God existed long before it possessed a complete Old or New Testament. The spoken Word of promise preceded the written Word. The oral words of prophets and apostles were the means of communicating God's will to men before we had the written Word. "The oral Word and the written Word are not in contradiction," says Werner Elert, a distinguished theologian.

VII. Preservation and Translation

No book has been so carefully preserved as the Bible. The scribes who copied the manuscripts (before printing was invented) were exacting and careful workmen. This was all the more necessary because the early manuscripts were without punctuation and letter followed letter with no spacing between the words. The original Hebrew script was without the vowel marks which are now part of the Hebrew text. To help the reader, these vowel marks were added by the Masoretes, a group of Biblical scholars who lived A. D. 500—1000. Their aim and that of earlier scribes was the exact preservation of the Old Testament text.

The original manuscripts (autographs) are of course no longer at hand, and so the question is often asked: Do we have a reliable text? Here the witness of the Dead Sea Scrolls found at Qumran is very significant. Some 40,000 inscribed fragments have been discovered since 1947 in a number of caves. Some 500 books have been reconstructed from them. About 100 of these books are from the Old Testament. All the books in the Old Testament, except the Book of Esther, are represented in these findings. The two Isaiah scrolls found at Qumran are 1,000 years older than any other known Old Testament scrolls. These scrolls from the second century B. C. are a good test of the accuracy of the Isaiah we have now in our

Bibles. Scholars tell us there is no major point of difference.

Sir Frederick Kenyon, director of the British Museum and himself a Biblical scholar, said: "The Christian can take the whole Bible in his hand and say without fear or hesitation that he holds in it the true Word of God handed down without essential loss from generation to generation throughout the centuries." (A. W. Adams, *Our Bible and the Ancient Manuscripts*)

The same thing can be said about Bible translations. F. C. Grant in his introduction to the Revised Standard Version of the New Testament wrote in 1946: "No doctrine of the Christian faith has been affected by the revision, for the simple reason that, out of thousands of variant readings in the manuscripts, none has turned up thus far that requires a revision of the Christian faith." Here too we see the hand of God in the preservation of His Word.

The amazing story of the translation of the whole Bible or the New Testament or individual books, first into the languages of the Near East and Mediterranean world, then into more European languages, is thrilling. But space in this book does not permit its inclusion. By 1968 the Bible or a portion of it had appeared in 1,200 languages and dialects. Bible translation teams are at work in almost all parts of the world. Since the first book (a Latin Bible — the Vulgate) came off the first printing press in 1455, the printing of the Bible has continued in a constantly increasing number of languages.

We may capsule this chapter on the nature and form of the Bible in the words of Edward Blair: "It is fair to say that the Bible contains one long story that embraces the whole universe and all time. It deals with God's attempt to bring into being a people with whom He might enter into intimate, holy fellowship, and the realization of this purpose at last through Jesus Christ. The Bible clearly contains no haphazard collection of miscellaneous books, but rather books that are related in some way to a single theme — the saving work of God." (*The Bible and You*, p. 17)

FOR FURTHER STUDY

Sunday:
John 5:39-43
John 20:30-31
2 Timothy 3:15-17

Carefully read these passages. Then record in a paragraph in your notebook what they teach regarding the purpose of the Scriptures.

Monday: *Psalm 19*	Note the comparison with "the book of nature" and "the Law (book) of the Lord." What does God's Word do for the believing reader?
Tuesday: *1 Peter 1* *2 Peter 1*	Read these two chapters and in your notebook list the things they teach with regard to origin of both Old and New Testaments.
Wednesday: *Acts 8:4-5* *Acts 20:32* *Ephesians 1:13* *Colossians 1:5*	In each passage identify the precise meaning of the term Word from the context, and put your findings in your notebook.
Thursday: *Ephesians 3:1-6*	What does this passage say about revelation given to prophets and apostles? Dig out all the facts in these verses, and record them in your notebook.
Friday: *Romans 1:19-20* *Romans 2:14-15*	What part do nature (creation) and conscience (God's law written in the heart) have in revealing to all mankind the existence of God?
Saturday: *Isaiah 55*	Read this description of the effect of the gracious Word of God, and in your notebook put down the messages it gives you.

References

Bruce, F. F. *The Books and the Parchments.* Westwood, N. J.: Revell, 1963. 288 pp. Excellent scholarship; recognized authority in the field.

Introduction to the Bible, Vol. 1 of *The Layman's Bible Commentary.* Foreman, Kelly, Rhodes, Metzger, Miller. Richmond: John Knox Press, 1959.

Lightfoot, Neil R. *How We Got the Bible.* Grand Rapids: Baker, 1965. 128 pp. A must for the teacher; suggest that class members purchase it also.

Manley, G. T. *The New Bible Handbook.* Chicago: Inter-Varsity Fellowship, 1950.

Chapter 8

75 TRANSLATIONS OF NEW TESTAMENT

Understanding the Bible

Introduction

The treasurer of Ethiopia was returning from Jerusalem. While riding in his chariot he was reading the book which we know as Isaiah. Suddenly a man came up to his chariot and asked the question, "Do you understand what you are reading?" He replied, "How can I, except someone explain it to me?" The man who spoke first was the evangelist Philip. He explained that the chapter the man was reading (Isaiah 53) was fulfilled in Christ, the promised Messiah. (Acts 8:26-40)

Because the Bible has been misused, misinterpreted, and misunderstood, many people down through the ages have asked the same question: How shall we understand the Bible? Though it has some difficult passages, almost all of it is understandable to the reader who will approach it with faith and an open mind. While the Bible is an ancient book, it is relevant to life in every age. In a very unique sense it is contemporary.

With the help of the Holy Spirit you too can understand this most remarkable book. It touches life at every level. It is the means God used to preserve what He revealed through prophets and apostles to His people in various ages. It is the fountain of our greatest knowledge. While it contains important history, tested wisdom, sublime poetry, and much moral teaching, it is chiefly the book that makes men wise unto salvation through faith in Jesus Christ.

Christ is the center of the Old and New Testaments. A proper interpretation of Scripture is therefore *Christological,* that is, it leads to a greater understanding of Jesus Christ, the Savior. This is clear from Jesus' own use of the Old Testament (John 5:39; Luke 24:25-27, 44-47) and from the express statements of New Testament writers (John 20:30-31; 2 Timothy 3:15; Hebrews 1:1-2; 1 Peter 1:10-11).

Basic Factors
for Understanding and Interpreting the Bible

Before we understand a book we must page through it to learn what kind of a book it is. A glance through a book of history or geography or mathematics or science will tell us at once its distinctive nature. The character of a book will in a sense determine our approach to it. We read a book of fiction quite differently than a textbook on astronomy. In this chapter we shall take up 10 basic concepts that should always be kept in mind when we read and interpret the Bible. Some of these have already been referred to in previous chapters. Here we look at the preliminaries before we go into the specifics of interpreting the Bible.

I. We Work with a Translation

In establishing Christian doctrine, the church has always considered the Hebrew (Old Testament) and Greek (New Testament) texts to be decisive. This is as it should be. No translation can take the place of the original, as every translator from one language to another knows. However, God wants the Gospel to get into all the world (Matthew 28:19; Mark 16:15). Translations permit modern man to get the message God intends for him. Fortunately all the generally accepted Bible translations faithfully preserve the doctrines conveyed in the original.

Today we have many fine new English translations based on the most reliable ancient manuscripts and on the latest Biblical research. Thus the modern reader can get a sharper understanding of the intended sense of the original Greek and Hebrew.

The Bible student therefore begins by making sure that the chapter, paragraph, or verse he is reading gives the essential message of the original text. At this point, comparing a number of English translations is very helpful.

II. God Speaks in Human Language

It was St. Augustine who said it is no more possible for finite man to comprehend the infinite God than for a child to dip the ocean into a hole he has made in the sand. God nevertheless found a way to speak His thoughts to the mind of man. He accommodated Himself to the limitations of human language. Jesus used parables from daily experience to teach divine truth. Everywhere the Bible uses "word pictures." God is described as a loving Father with deep concern for all of His children. Christian truth is given to us in human terms. Thus, for instance, in the Book of Revelation the glories of heaven are described in the rich imagery of "streets of gold" and "gates of pearl." Even more wonderful is the fact that God sent His Son into the world in human form to communicate with men. (John 1:14; Hebrews 1:1-2)

The Scripture lets God speak in human language. What is more, the writers speak as people then spoke, using their language idioms, their methods of telling a story, and their ways of joining words together to express their thoughts. This means that we must put ourselves in the writer's shoes and recapture the thought he wished to convey by the words or illustrations he used. Knowledge of Bible times (over many centuries) is important for understanding Scripture, just as we need to know English expressions of Shakespeare's time to understand Shakespeare.

III. The Bible Uses Various Literary Forms

In many instances the literary form has a direct bearing on the meaning of the text. We distinguish prose from poetry, narrative from drama. The Bible contains all of these forms. It would be a mistake to interpret all the Book of Revelation literally, since much of it is figurative in the extreme. There is elaborate symbolism in Zechariah, Ezekiel, and Daniel. By interpreting them with slavish literalism we get a meaningless jumble of ideas. The same is true of the Lord's teachings in parables. Nothing is gained and much is lost by applying a method that does not fit the literary form. At many points there is a merging of forms, with symbolism ceasing and common speech beginning. This is by no means always at once apparent.

It is an advantage to use an English Bible in which the poetic sections are shown as poetry. Most modern poetry is based on "sound and rhythm," while Hebrew poetry is based on "thought and rhythm." The latter is based on parallelism rather than rhyme. A verse will contain lines that merely *repeat* the thought in different words, or lines that *advance* the thought with a new element, or lines which state the very *opposite*.

We use one approach in reading poetry, another in reading narratives (Esther, Ruth, Jonah), and still another as we come to the great drama of Job with its discussion of the problem of human suffering. Proverbs and Ecclesiastes are examples of the wisdom literature of the Bible. Here almost every sentence may contain a new thought. The epistles of Paul are *letters* in a very real sense, containing chiefly instructional material. Much of the Old Testament, as also of the gospels and Acts in the New Testament, is historical in form. "Literary form governs the meaning of sentences and therefore the interpreter must be sensitive to the implications of the literary form." (Bernard Ramm, *Protestant Biblical Interpretation*, p. 139)

IV. Time and Setting

※   Every book of the Bible needs to be interpreted in the light of the time in which it was written, the circumstances which brought about the writing, the problems and needs that occasioned it. We see how important this is, for example, when we study the letters of the apostle Paul. We will gain much if we know for whom, by whom, and to whom a book was written. An interpretation that does not consider the setting in life *(Sitz im Leben)* is usually invalid.

This is where the findings of archeology, the history of surrounding nations, the customs of the people of the time contribute to a better understanding of a given Biblical book. Many phrases will be incomprehensible to us unless we know something about the customs of the time. Jesus illustrated a major point when He said that men do not put new wine into old bottles (Matthew 9:17). The bottles people used for carrying wine were made of animal skins. No wonder a person would not put new wine in old bottles! Many of the psalms, for instance, the penitential psalms of David (32; 51), are best understood when related to an episode in the life of the writer. Sometimes the caption at the head of a psalm gives us the clue. The Bible student therefore must ask: When was this written? and then try to determine the occasion, situation, or setting of a chapter or paragraph. This can be gained from commentaries or study Bibles which supply introductions to the books of the Bible.

V. The Bible Is Unfolding Revelation

As we read from Genesis to Revelation we find that the Scriptures reveal more and more of what God wants man to know. God does not give a full-blown picture of Himself or of His will for man in any one book of the Bible. God's revelation moves forward toward fuller completion until it reaches its climax in the New Testament, particularly in the person of Jesus Christ (Hebrews 1:1-2). The whole Book of Hebrews is an illustration of this. What God promised through the symbolic rites of the Old Testament are only "the shadow of the substance," which is Christ!

> Let no one pass judgment on you in questions of food and drink or with regard to a festival or a new moon or a sabbath. These are only a shadow of what is to come; but the substance belongs to Christ. *Colossians 2:16-17*

Old Testament history, types, symbols, rules, and promises give way to New Testament realization. It is for this reason also that Christians very properly occupy themselves more with the New Testament than with the Old, although the two are inseparable and both merit close study.

The Bible, in both the Old and the New Testament, presents the same God, who revealed more and more of Himself to His people as time went on. This does not mean that the Old Testament is unclear or inferior, but simply that it is like the sunrise, while the New Testament is like the blazing sunlight of noonday. The New Testament marks the fulfillment of the Old. Jesus recognized this principle when He said He came not to abolish the Law but to fulfill it (Matthew 5:17). Then He gave the higher, fuller meaning of certain commandments (Matthew 5:21-48). The principle of clarification, in keeping with the disciples' progressive understanding, is stated by Jesus: "I have yet many things to say to you, but you cannot bear them now." (John 16:12)

SHOW US JESUS!

VI. Keep Scripture's Specific Purpose in Mind

The Bible is a book with a purpose. That purpose is to reveal God's grace and loving concern for the salvation of all mankind. It tells the story of redemption in great breadth, all the way from Genesis to Revelation. This is the aim of the Scripture, and sound interpretation must never lose sight of this aim. "Consequently, it is a serious and misleading error to regard the Bible as a source book on science, philosophy, or any subject other than its central theme." (Frank E. Gaebelein, *Exploring the Bible*, p. 190)

Bible scholars agree that there is a proper scope of Scripture. It is folly to insist that Scripture is a single compilation of all scientific knowledge or a complete historical record of ancient man. It is neither of these. It is much more. It is the authoritative record of God's dealings with humanity, to the end that man might be reconciled to God. This does not mean that the Bible is not reliable when it speaks on history or science. The spade of the archeologist is constantly proving that it is reliable. All the while God's purpose is not to teach history or science but to reveal the things which man could never seek out through the exercise of his own reasoning and inventive faculties. These God in His infinite wisdom set forth completely and finally in Scripture.

LAW IN NEW TESTAMENT

VII. The Bible Teaches Law and Gospel

The Bible is *not* "just another book of religious ethics." It has two major teachings: Law and Gospel. With the Law (essentially the Ten Commandments) God exposes man's shortcomings, failings, disobediences, and sins as departures from His will. Through the Law God awakens in us a sense of sinfulness and shows us our need of forgiveness. Through the Gospel He offers and conveys to us His grace and forgiveness in Christ. It was grace that caused God the Father to plan for the salvation of all mankind. His plan was implemented when He sent His Son "in the fullness of time" to work out redemption "through His blood." God gives the Holy Spirit to apply this free salvation to human hearts by means of the Gospel. (Ephesians 1:3-14)

LAW:
① SELF RIGHTEOUS
② VERY DISTRAINING
③ DRIVES YOU TO GOSPEL

92

The teaching of God's law on the sinfulness of men is found everywhere in the Old Testament. No reader can miss it. The Old Testament is not confined to the Law but also contains much Gospel. The grace and mercy of God and His readiness to forgive all who come to Him is taught in many places and in many ways: in direct statements, in parables, in symbols. In the Old Testament, sacri- ✳ ficial types and symbols pictured the atonement of sins to be made through the suffering and death of the promised Messiah. God's great acts, such as the deliverance of His people from the bondage of Egypt, teach His grace and mercy. In these the Christian interpreter finds the Gospel message, as certainly the author of Hebrews did, particularly in chapters 8 – 10. Note the words of Jesus:

> As Moses lifted up the serpent in the wilderness, so must the Son of Man be lifted up, that whoever believes in Him may have eternal life.　　　　　　　　*John 3:14-15*

In the New Testament we find both Law (God's demands) and Gospel (God's grace) in every one of its books. In such chapters as Matthew 5 – 7 (Sermon on the Mount) our Lord interprets the spiritual demands of the Law and describes those who by faith have become "new creatures." In such parables as the story of the Prodigal Son (Luke 15), and in such chapters as John 3 and Romans 5, we have a clear revelation of the Gospel.

In full harmony with such Law-and-Gospel teaching is the central teaching of Christianity: justification by grace through faith in Jesus Christ. It is clearly defined in Romans and Galatians:

> We hold that a man is justified by faith apart from works of Law.　　　　　　　　*Romans 3:28*

> We ourselves, who are Jews by birth and not Gentile sinners, yet who know that a man is not justified by works of the Law but through faith in Jesus Christ, even we have believed in Christ Jesus, in order to be justified by faith in Christ and not by works of the Law, because by works of the Law shall no one be justified.　　*Galatians 2:16*

Equally important is the principle that Law and Gospel are not to be confused. What is Law should not be turned into Gospel, and Gospel must not be made into a Law. In his book *Protestant*

Biblical Interpretation Bernard Ramm writes: "Luther taught that we must carefully distinguish Law and Gospel in the Bible, and this was one of Luther's principal *hermeneutical* rules. Any fusion of the Law and Gospel was wrong (Catholics and Reformed who make the Gospel a new law), and any repudiation of the Law was wrong (antinomianism). The Law was God's Word about human sin, human imperfection, and whose purpose was to drive us to our knees under a burden of guilt. The Gospel is God's grace and power to save. Hence we must never in interpreting the Scriptures confuse these two different activities of God or teachings of Holy Scripture." (P. 57)

VIII. Christian Doctrine Must Be Based on Clear Passages

Everything essential to salvation is so clearly revealed in Scripture that the average person can find it. The sinfulness of man is written on almost every page of Scripture (Genesis 3 – 11; Romans 1 – 3; 1 John 1:5-10; etc.). The grace of God and His free salvation are expressed hundreds of times in the Old Testament: in God's mighty acts of deliverance, in the entire sacrificial system, and in specific pronouncements and promises (Isaiah 1:8; 53:5; Jeremiah 31:31-34; etc.). It pervades the whole New Testament (John 3; Romans 5; 2 Corinthians 5; etc.). So it is with every essential doctrine: the deity of Christ (John 5), the resurrection of Christ (1 Corinthians 15), the doctrine of the church (Ephesians; 1 Corinthians 12; Romans 12), justification by faith (Romans 3; Galatians 2; etc.), Christian life and mission (Matthew 5 – 7; Ephesians 4 – 6; James 1 – 5; Matthew 28; 1 Peter 2), and eternal life (John 3).

Confusion in Christian teaching is largely traceable to the unscholarly use of Scripture passages to support human speculation or interpretations. Doctrinal conclusions need to be based on those larger segments of Scripture and those specific passages which are clear and readily understood by the average reader. For example, salvation by grace is explicitly taught in Ephesians 1:3-14; 2:8-9; Romans 3:24; 11:6; Titus 3:7, and similar passages. To stress care in the use of God's Word, the apostle asserts this principle:

> Do your best to present yourself to God as one approved, a workman who has no need to be ashamed, rightly handling the Word of truth.
> _2 Timothy 2:15_

Of course, there are some obscure passages in both the Old and New Testament. We may never be able to fully explain, for example, who Melchizedek was (Genesis 14:18; Psalm 110:4; Hebrews 7:1-17), or what is meant by "baptism for the dead" (1 Corinthians 15:29), for in this life we "know only in part" (1 Corinthians 13:9). The footnotes in the RSV frequently call attention to alternate translations or to obscurities in the Hebrew or Greek text. But let it always be remembered that the way of salvation is so clear that a child can understand it. At the same time the Scripture is so challenging that we can remain students of it as long as we live. Someone has put this into a parabolic saying: "The Scripture is a river in which a lamb can wade and an elephant swim."

IX. Don't Carry Your Meaning into Scripture

The interpreter must keep the role of _discoverer_ and not become the _inventor._ The important question for him is: What does the whole passage in its total setting say to us today? We are not to carry our dogma or opinion into the Scripture but let Christian doctrine grow out of Scripture. This is to say the Bible must remain the source and norm of Christian teaching and faith. Much damage has been done by subjective, opinionated interpretations of the Scripture. The Bible student must remain objective in his study. For this reason the inductive approach in Bible study is so important, because it draws general principles from a careful consideration of particular instances in the Biblical text itself. Inductive means beginning with particular facts in the text and drawing a conclusion from them. The interpreter operates with the discoverable facts in the Bible, not unlike the way the scientist deals with data in his field.

X. The Christian Use of Scripture

The "Christian" use of the Bible is given to us in some detail

95

in 2 Timothy 3:15-17, namely, (1) for instruction in salvation, (2) for teaching, (3) for reproof, (4) for correction, and (5) for training in righteousness. Scripture calls us to repentance with its Law and restores us to newness of life with its Gospel. It charts the way for righteousness and godly living; it equips man for a life of good works and service. This passage more than any other determines the Christian use of the Bible.

There is a tendency to misuse the Bible by a radical liberalism which rejects the basic teachings of Christianity and by a false literalism which confuses Law and Gospel. Both do a disservice to the proper interpretation of Scripture. Paul calls on us to "rightly handle the Word of truth." Peter too warns, with respect to the misuse of Biblical writings:

> So also our beloved brother Paul wrote to you according to the wisdom given him, speaking of you as he does in all his letters. There are some things in them hard to understand, which the ignorant and unstable twist to their own destruction, as they do other Scriptures.   *2 Peter 3:15-16*

The apostle adds: "Therefore, beloved, knowing this beforehand, beware lest you be carried away with the error of lawless men and lose your own stability. But grow in the grace and knowledge of our Lord and Savior Jesus Christ." (Vv. 17-18)

In this chapter we have looked at basic presuppositions as the underlying factors for understanding the Bible. In the next chapter we examine four fundamental rules of hermeneutics, the science of Biblical interpretation.

FOR FURTHER STUDY

Sunday   Reread this chapter. What new understandings did it give you? Write them in your notebook. Reexamine 2 Timothy 3:14-17. How do you personally apply the five practical functions of Scripture when you hear, read, or study God's Word?

Monday   Read Matthew 12 and Romans 12 in the King James Version of the Bible (first printed in 1611), and list the expressions which have become archaic or obsolete and which no longer communicate to youth today. Then read the chapters in one or more recent translations: Revised Standard Version, Phillips translation, New English Bible, etc. What help did you find with the words you listed from KJV?

Tuesday Read the parable of the Prodigal Son (Luke 15), and change it from a parable into a statement of the truths it teaches. Whom do the persons signify? What do the actions represent and teach? Is it more forceful in story form?

Wednesday List the symbolic or picture words used in Psalm 46. What does each picture word mean? Would you prefer "picture-less" language in the Psalms?

Thursday Read Ecclesiastes 1. What does it say? How would you classify its contents (history, teaching, meditation, philosophy, introspection, review of life)?

Friday In what sense is the Bible (Old and New Testament) an "unfolding" revelation? What does this mean for the interpreter?

Saturday Why is the differentiation between Law and Gospel such a basic principle in understanding the Bible? What happens when you give all Scripture equal significance? mix Law and Gospel?

References

Colson, Howard P. *Preparing to Teach the Bible*. Nashville: Convention Press, 1959. 148 pp.

deDietrich, Suzanne. *God's Unfolding Purpose: A Guide to the Study of the Bible*. Philadelphia: Westminster Press, 1960. 287 pp.

Manley, G. T. *The New Bible Handbook*. Chicago: Inter-Varsity Christian Fellowship, 1950. 465 pp.

Ramm, Bernard. *Protestant Biblical Interpretation*. Natick, Mass.: W. A. Wilde Co., 1956. 274 pp.

Chapter 9

Basic Principles of Interpretation

Through the prophets and apostles God still speaks to us today. We understand God's will when we keep in mind the true nature of the Bible and how it speaks to our situation. In Chapter 8 we considered 10 general factors the Bible student should keep in mind. Let us look at them again.

We work with a translation
God speaks to us in human language
The Bible uses various literary forms
Time and setting of each book are important
The Bible is an "unfolding" revelation
Keep Scripture's specific purpose in mind
The Bible teaches Law and Gospel
Christian doctrine must be based on clear passages
Don't carry your own meaning into Scripture
There is a Christian use of the Bible

Before proceeding to specific rules for interpreting the Bible, let us get clear on the purposes of sound interpretation. Briefly stated they are:

— to understand the words of Scripture and the message they convey
— to bridge the gap of culture between the world of the Bible and the world of today
— to distinguish between the voice of God and the voice of man (inside the Bible and outside the Bible)
— to have a sure foundation for Christian faith and life

These reasons have compelled Christians through the centuries to seek interpretation that is theologically and Biblically sound and intellectually honest and valid.

The Bible itself indicates the need for interpretation. John, writing for non-Jewish readers, interprets Rabbi, Messiah, Cephas, and Siloam (John 1:38, 41-42; 9:7). Luke tells us what the name Dorcas means (Acts 9:36). Jesus meeting the disciples on the road to Emmaus "interpreted" and "opened up" some Old Testament Scriptures to help them "understand" why they should accept His resurrection (Luke 24:27, 32, 45). Paul did the same for the Thessalonians (Acts 17:2-3, 11). Aquila and Priscilla "expounded" to Apollos the way of God "more accurately" (Acts 18:26). Already in Jesus' time the rabbis had developed schools of interpretation which, however, at times overlaid the text with private opinions.

Many principles for interpreting the Bible have been advanced by various scholars. They can be drawn together in a few major categories. We shall look at five aspects:

> Interpreting the Scripture grammatically
> Letting Scripture interpret Scripture
> Observing the law of context
> Explaining Scripture in harmony with itself
> Recognizing figures of speech

The rules of Biblical interpretation should recognize (1) the nature of communication through human language and (2) the nature of the Holy Scriptures as a unique book.

I. Interpreting Scripture Grammatically

We begin by treating Scripture as we would any other book. This means interpreting the Scripture *grammatically*, according to sentence structure and word meaning. Nothing should be extracted from the text which ignores the rules of grammar. No statement normally has more than one intended meaning. No prudent, conscientious man intends that a diversity of meanings should be attached to what he writes. The usage of the word at the time of writing is normally decisive.

As in reading any book, we read sentences in the Scripture with subjects, verbs, and predicates. We distinguish between nouns and verbs, adjectives and adverbs, prepositions and conjunctions. The "wherefores" make important connections. The little word "so" in John 3:16 helps us understand the depth of God's love. The word "was" in John 1:1 implies the previous existence of Christ.

The actual meaning of the words must be grasped first. If we are reading one of Jesus' parables or John's visions, we will soon find that the words have a figurative meaning that goes beyond what first comes to the eye. This is not true of the Bible only. It's true of much of literature in practically every language. It is true of the stories of Hans Christian Andersen.

Prophetic statements in the Old Testament reach beyond the time of utterance to the time of fulfillment. In some instances they look to special fulfillment at a later time. A case in point is Hosea 11:1: "Out of Egypt I called My son." The prophet refers to the Children of Israel delivered by the hand of God from Egypt's bondage. But Matthew 2:15 gives a new interpretation, applying the prophecy to Israel's greatest Son, Jesus Christ, who as a child was taken to Egypt to escape the massacre of Herod and later returned to Palestine to carry out the mission His Father gave Him.

In ancient times there existed various schools of interpretation. Both Jewish and early Christian teachers used the allegorical method. By way of example, they found four meanings in the name Jerusalem. (1) Literally, they said, it means a city in Judea, (2) allegorically, it means the church militant, (3) morally, it means every faithful soul, and (4) mystically, it means the heavenly Jerusalem. Imagine the bewilderment (rather than enlightenment) such a fanciful method fostered. First used by the Jews in Alexandria, Egypt, from about 160 B. C., it continued for more than 1,500 years in some parts of the church. This method obscures rather than clarifies.

Luther insisted that the literal sense of the word is basic, that only compelling evidence in the context permits departure from it. Even a figurative sense cannot be established until the normal, conversational, literal sense has been established.

While the literal, grammatical sense is the starting point, the intended sense is the thing that is decisive. We must ask: What is clearly the intended sense of the author as he employs words? In most cases he conveys the literal dictionary sense of words. In some cases the writer uses a word as a figure. For instance, Christ calls upon His followers to be the "salt" of the earth, the "light" of the world, and the "leaven" of society. In each case the intended sense is clear: to permeate, influence, affect people by Christian faith and life. Note how Jesus indicated the intended sense when He used "leaven" figuratively. (Matthew 16:5-12)

While good interpretation finds the one intended meaning, the application of a verse can vary. Applications, however, should be made only after the basic, originally intended sense has first been established. They must not contradict the intended sense. Otherwise the real meaning of the Scripture is hidden by farfetched applications. Put in another way, the "then and there" meaning (interpretation of text) must first be established before we are ready for the "here and now" meaning (application).

The Bible student must follow the rules of language, respect the literary style, consider the context in which a word is used, and determine the use of the word at the time of writing. The first general rule then is: *Take a word of Scripture in its normal, literal, and grammatical sense* (place in the sentence) *to find its intended meaning.* From this we depart only when the verses preceding and following compel a figurative understanding.

II. The Scripture Is Its Own Best Interpreter

In his second letter Peter speaks of the prophetic Word as being sure, as shining like a lamp in a dark place, and then adds these words:

> First of all you must understand this, that no prophecy of Scripture is a matter of one's own interpretation, because no prophecy ever came by the impulse of man, but men moved by the Holy Spirit spoke from God.
>
> *2 Peter 1:20-21*

To avoid purely subjective and human interpretations, the Reformation leaders very properly emphasized the principle that *Scripture alone* establishes doctrine; that it is the source of our faith, as used by the Holy Spirit; and that it is the norm by which we are to judge all teaching. Without this principle the church becomes the victim of variant theological interpretations and of her own self-deceptions. Outside the Scripture we really have no place to stand. Our faith and life are not to rest on tradition, speculative philosophy, human opinion, or mere man-made traditions but on the clear words of Scripture. Jesus asked the scribes and Pharisees: "Why do you transgress the commandment of God for the sake of your tradition?" (Matthew 15:3). The apostle Paul warns: "See to it that no one makes a prey of you by philosophy and empty deceit, according to human tradition." (Colossians 2:8)

The words of Psalm 31:1, "In Thy righteousness deliver me," took on new significance when Luther compared them with passages in Romans.

> The righteousness of God has been manifested apart from Law, although the Law and the Prophets bear witness to it, the righteousness of God through faith in Jesus Christ for all who believe. *Romans 3:21-22*

> What does the Scripture say? "Abraham believed God, and it was reckoned to him as righteousness." Now to one who works, his wages are not reckoned as a gift but as his due. And to one who does not work but trusts Him who justifies the ungodly, his faith is reckoned as righteousness. *Romans 4:3-5*

> Since we are justified by faith, we have peace with God through our Lord Jesus Christ. *Romans 5:1*

This illustrates the principle of "letting Scripture interpret Scripture."

An interpretation given to a passage must stand in the light of the whole Scripture. Successive pronouncements in Scripture on a single subject may broaden and enlarge its scope. The comparison of one passage with other passages should include whole books as well as major sections and verses. We get a fuller understanding of the miracles and parables of our Lord as we compare the accounts of Matthew, Mark, Luke, and John. We get a better understanding of the teaching of Paul as we take into consideration all that he wrote, comparing, for instance, such companion books as Romans and Galatians, or referring to passages on justification by grace through faith as they occur in all of his letters.

We frequently speak of this as using the parallel passages or cross references as found in the margins of most study Bibles or in the footnotes. We distinguish between *real* cross references, in which the *same thought* is meant by the word used, and *apparent* cross references, where the *same word* is used but in a *different* sense. Thus Paul uses "law" in various senses, for instance, in Romans and Galatians. In all cases the context must decide the meaning of "law"; we must determine whether the Decalog, Levitical laws, or civil law is meant.

Note the following examples:

a. *Word* Parallels: Note the difference in the meaning of "faith" as used in Romans 5:1 (specific) and in Hebrews 11:1 (general).

b. *Thought* Parallels: Observe that in Luke 21:33 and 1 Peter 1:25 not only the same word is used but also the same thought is implied.

c. Parallel *Sections:* Compare Philippians 2 with Hebrews 2. How are they alike? What are the points of difference?

d. Parallel *Books:* Ephesians tells us about the church of which Christ is the Head. Colossians also speaks of Christ as the Head of church and universe, but emphasizes more the person of Christ. There are many similarities in these two books, but also some differences.

Go to a commentary, theological word book, or Bible dictionary to learn from the experts in what sense a word is used in a particular verse.

Occasionally the student finds a dark or obscure passage. (In some instances a footnote in the RSV will indicate why the translation is uncertain.) How shall he deal with it? The general rule is to interpret the less clear passages in the light of passages or verses which deal with the same subject more clearly and completely. Thus we should not interpret Revelation 20 (with its reference to a thousand years) without taking into consideration the Lord's teaching on the Last Times in Matthew 24 and Mark 13. Figurative passages can be understood better when seen in the light of passages which deal with the same truth directly and literally.

The general overarching rule to "let Scripture interpret Scripture" includes also that "everything in Scripture should be understood in the light of the Gospel and the teachings of our Lord."

103

III. Observe the Law of Context

Practically every public speaker has suffered from the newspaper reporter who has torn a statement out of the fuller development given by the speaker. The result is a distorted message and frequently the beginning of controversy. Practically any religious error can be supported by phrases from Scripture torn out of their connection.

※ The word "context" refers to the total setting of a verse or paragraph. This means that a verse must be seen in the light of the preceding and following verses. A paragraph is to be seen in relation to other paragraphs in the chapter, and a chapter in relation to the entire book of which it is a part. We call this the *immediate context*.

※ The *remote context* includes more. It takes in not only the entire book and its historical setting but also other works by the same author (for instance, all of Paul's letters). It embraces the whole Old or New Testament of which it is a part. A passage or book of either Testament has relationships to the whole Testament and to the whole Bible.

Keep in mind the interrelatedness of Scripture portions. This is important, because a text without reference to its context can easily become a pretext. In this case something other than the basic, intended first meaning is given to a passage. This is not sound Biblical interpretation. We misuse Scripture verses when we detach them from their context. This is what Peter meant when he spoke of some who "twist [the Scripture] to their own destruction" (2 Peter 3:16). Isolated passages divorced from their context can be misleading.

Here are a few ways of expressing this law of context to help you remember it:

(1) *Interpret the part in the light of the whole; and interpret the whole in the light of the part.*
(2) *Never tear a passage out of its connection.*
(3) *What a word means in any given sentence can only be determined by its immediate context in that sentence.*

104

Every passage has its own setting, and the meaning of the same word can be determined only by the particular sentence in which it is used. Thus, for example, "old" takes on various meanings from its surroundings. What different meanings of "old" do you see in the following phrases?

old man
old newspaper
three days old
old friend
Old Testament?

Examples:

a. What happens when you separate Philippians 2:12 from Philippians 2:13? Explain.

b. How is Matthew 18:21-22 illuminated by the parable of the King's Servant, vv. 23-35?

c. Read John 5:39. (Compare RSV with KJV.) Is the word "search" an imperative or a declarative word as here used? Determine this by reading the entire section, vv. 30-47.

IV. Interpret the Scripture in Harmony with Itself

This rule builds on the premise that the Scripture is a unity. Just as the scientist examining the human body sees the relation of one organ to another and of one function to another in diagnosing a person's illness, so the good interpreter takes into consideration the whole written Word that God has preserved for us. In other words, the Old and New Testaments are related to each other as mold to medallion. They cannot and should not be divorced.

To observe this close relationship, look for the word "fulfilled" in the following passages and write in the Old Testament reference (as given in the margin or footnote of your Bible):

Matthew 1:22-23 _ISA 7:14_   12:17-18 _____
          2:14-15 _HOS 11:1 EX.4:22_   13:13-14 _____
          2:17-18 _JER 31:15_   13:34-35 _____
          4:14-15 _ISA 9:1,2_   21:4-5 _____
          8:17 _ISA 53:4_   27:9 _____
                                    27:35 _____

105

Just as the Old and New Testaments are to be seen in relation to each other, so also Law and Gospel in both Testaments should be seen as related. Where this is ignored, the interpreter is in danger of teaching mere religiosity or moralisms instead of the basic message of the Old and New Testaments: sin and grace.

Jesus Christ unites the two Testaments. Therefore the Christian interpreter reads the Old Testament as one who knows that its rites, prophecies, and symbols have been fulfilled in Jesus Christ. This we learn from the manner in which Jesus and the apostles used the Old Testament. As we have already noted, the Book of Hebrews is a case in point. Scripture itself suggests a Christological interpretation of the Old Testament. (1 Peter 1:10-12)

To interpret the Bible in harmony with itself means that no passage should be interpreted contrary to clearly revealed doctrines of the Bible, or to put it another way, no interpretation is correct which contradicts a fundamental teaching of the Bible. This is called "The Rule of Faith" or "The Rule of Scripture."

People often report that they find contradictions in the Bible. Examine a few examples. Scripture clearly teaches that we are made right with God through faith in Jesus, the Redeemer. It also teaches that faith is never alone, that is, without its fruit of good works.

Read Galatians 2:16 and James 2:24.
Then read James 2:26 and Galatians 5:6.
Read 1 John 1:8-10 and 1 John 3:9.
Then read 1 John 3:23-24 and 3:10.

These last passages are in the same book, written by the same author. They should be interpreted in a *complementary* way, not in a contradictory manner.

Sometimes what seems to be a contradiction is a misidentification of subject matter.

Read Romans 8:38-39 and Hebrews 6:4-6.
Are the subjects in these two passages identical?
The context of Romans 8 is God's faithfulness.
The context of Hebrews 6 is man's apostasy.

106

V. How to Understand Figurative Parts of Scripture

All living language has figures of speech. Figurative language and poetic imagery enrich meaning. The Bible uses metaphors, similes, parables, types, and a great deal of symbolism. The reader must recognize when such figures of speech are used in the text. The reader is justified in departing from the literal meaning when the text and context demand this. Usually the Scripture itself gives us the signal with such phrases as "the kingdom of God is *like* . . . ." (See Matthew 13:24, 31, 33, 44-45, 47.)

Jesus was a master at teaching with parables. Parables can be properly interpreted or overinterpreted. The principle is to find the major point of comparison. To go beyond this major point or key can become imaginative speculation. Scholars warn against making a parable "walk on all fours" instead of finding the basic central message it wishes to convey.

1. A parable is a comparative narrative which uses an earthly incident to illustrate a spiritual truth. It puts two things side by side. Someone has said, "Look for the key. It usually hangs close to the door." He meant to say: Look for the signals, find the clues. For instance, the key to the three parables in Luke 15 is found in verses 1 and 2.
2. An allegory is more difficult to detect and interpret. It usually teaches a moral or spiritual lesson in terms of a historical incident. Galatians 4:21-31 is a good example.
3. A type is usually an Old Testament character or function used as a symbol or pattern of a New Testament fact. The Passover is a type of the Lord's Supper. Old Testament sacrifices are a type of Christ, the Lamb of God, sacrificed for us. The high priest is a type of Christ and His functions. The holy of holies of the tabernacle or temple is a type of heaven. The Book of Hebrews is largely theological interpretation of Old Testament persons and functions as prophetic symbols or types of Christ. Read Hebrews 8, 9, and 10 for examples.

In addition we must remember that Scripture, like most literature, employs many literary forms. Words like "enlighten" and "convert" are metaphors. Both involve a picture. A metaphor is a comparison of two things without the use of "as" or "like."

A simile is a comparison using the signal "like" or "as."

A paradox is two assertions that seem to be contradictory.

A hyperbole is an overstatement, an intentional use of exaggeration.

A synecdoche uses a part for the whole, for instance, "bread" for "food."

Figures of speech make the Bible more interesting. Mere prose could not express as effectively the providence and care of our Lord as is done in the poetic imagery of Psalm 23. The seven "I am" statements in John's Gospel (for instance, "I am the Vine, you are the branches") are figures of speech. Each one enlarges our understanding of Christ. The worldwide healing power of the Gospel is given in picture form in Ezekiel 47, which describes the Gospel as four healing streams that flow from under the altar of God.

The serpent lifted up in the wilderness (Numbers 21) has Gospel significance as interpreted in John 3:14. The fall of man in Genesis 3 is further interpreted in Romans 5, which compares the "first man," Adam, and the "second Man," Jesus Christ. The term Lamb of God, applied in John 1:29 to our Lord, sheds new light on Leviticus, the book of Old Testament sacrifices.

Some symbolisms, of course, are difficult to understand, and interpretations will vary as to their suggested meanings. A single symbol may be used in Scripture in a variety of ways. Thus the lion figure is used to symbolize Israel (Genesis 49:9), Christ (Revelation 5:5), Satan (1 Peter 5:8), tyrants (2 Timothy 4:7), and enemies (Psalm 91:13).

In the following passages find the word which signals the use of a symbol, type, or comparison:

Matthew 13:31, 33 _____

Romans 5:14 _____

Galatians 4:24 _____

Hebrews 8:5 _____

1 Peter 3:21 (KJV) _____ (RSV) _____

VI. Read with Spiritual Discernment

Samuel Coleridge called attention to the importance of the Holy Spirit in reading and understanding the Bible with his famous saying: "The Bible without the Spirit is a sundial by moonlight." To understand what he meant, we need to look at 1 Corinthians 2:9-14. There we are told that the human eye and heart cannot conceive what God is pleased to reveal through the Spirit, because the Spirit searches everything, even the deep things of God. The apostle explains that only a person's spirit can know the thoughts within that person. So we cannot expect to know the thoughts of God except by the guidance of the Holy Spirit.

Christians have not the spirit of the world but the Spirit which is from God. This Spirit not only guides them into Biblical truth but also interprets spiritual truths to those who possess the Spirit. This is another way of saying that when the man of faith comes to God's Word, it will open before him its treasures of gold and silver and precious jewels, for Paul again says: "The unspiritual man does not receive the gifts of the Spirit of God, for they are folly to him, and he is not able to understand them because they are spiritually discerned." (1 Corinthians 2:14)

"The natural man comprehends natural things. His spiritual faculties are undeveloped to understand the things that are from above. Not until the natural man undergoes the regenerative change of conversion does he have the first prerequisite for an understanding of the great message of the Bible." (Gaebelein, p. 179)

Christ has promised this Spirit to us, saying: "How much more will the heavenly Father give His Holy Spirit to them that ask Him!" Thanks to the Spirit, the treasurer of Ethiopia learned to understand Isaiah 53 (Acts 8:25-40). With the Spirit's help you too can understand your Bible.

SUMMARY

1. Take the words of Scripture in their normal, literal, intended sense unless preceding or following verses compel a figurative understanding.
2. Let the Bible interpret itself. Do not read your opinions into it. One passage casts light on another, the clear verse on the

difficult. Use reference (parallel) passages, concordance, and dictionary.

3. Never tear a passage out of its connection.
4. No passage should be understood in a way that contradicts another clear statement of Scripture.
5. Interpret the Scripture historically (in the light of history).
6. Interpret the Scripture evangelically (in the light of the Gospel and the person of Christ).

FOR FURTHER STUDY

Sunday
Hebrews 5:11
to 6:3

What encouragement does this passage give the individual Christian for the serious study of God's Word? How does it encourage every believer to be also a teacher of the Scriptures?

Monday
James 1:
16-25

What does this passage teach about the role of God's Word in the Christian's life—his conversion, his regular use of the Word, his living by the Word?

Tuesday
1 Peter
2:1-10

How is the mission of every Christian described here? Meditate on your own acceptance of "the priesthood of all believers." What is the relation of spiritual growth to exercising your priesthood?

Wednesday
2 Peter
1:16-21

We who have the written, prophetic Word are in a sense more privileged than even the eyewitnesses of Christ. Why? What direction does it give us for becoming Christian interpreters of Scripture?

Thursday
Matthew
22:29-33
Mark 7:1-12

List the lessons these verses suggest for the use of the Scriptures. What point is Jesus driving home in this contrast between "tradition" and God's "commandment"?

Friday
Luke 24:
25-27, 32
Luke 24:
44-50

What principle of Biblical interpretation is Jesus illustrating here? What does it teach about the relationship between the Old Testament and Jesus' teaching ministry?

Saturday
Psalm 19

What two kinds of revelation does the writer speak of? What does the created world around us tell us about God? (Romans 1:18-20). Why is God's written Word a necessity? (Psalm 19:7-13). What guidance for your life did you find in verse 14?

References

Bohlmann, Ralph A. *Principles of Biblical Interpretation in the Lutheran Confessions.* St. Louis: Concordia Publishing House, 1968.

Colson, Howard P. *Preparing to Teach the Bible.* Nashville: Convention Press, 1959. 148 pp.

Mayer, Herbert T. *Interpreting the Holy Scriptures.* St. Louis: Concordia Publishing House, 1967. 120 pp.

Ramm, Bernard. *Protestant Biblical Interpretation.* Natick, Mass.: Wilde, 1956. 274 pp.

Chapter 10

Overview of the Old Testament

An aeroplane view of a mountain range of 39 distinct peaks, each a little different from the other, gives the geographer or mountain climber some impressions he could not get in any other way. He sees the whole structure, the peaks and valleys, the chief ridges between peaks. But he cannot see all the smaller details, all the gorges, all the jutting precipices and waterfalls.

A brief survey of the Old Testament does not permit an analysis of each book or attention to minute incidents. But it can outline the chief movements in the history of God's people, the main concepts in their worship and way of life, and the relationship of one movement to another in the working out of God's plan in historical events.

Seven such concepts are given in this chapter. They serve as guides for reading and understanding all 39 books of the Old Testament.

This chapter enables you to see Old Testament events in perspective. Most of us can recall isolated events and persons. Here we see them in relation to each other. Any chapter which condenses thousands of years into a few pages requires concentration. How may you proceed in this chapter? First, read it through without stopping to look up references in your Bible. Then read it a second time (perhaps one section each day). This time look up one or more key passages in each paragraph in addition to those printed out in the chapter, especially the New Testament references. Such careful reading will give you "the thread of the Old Testament."

I. The Prologue: The Beginning

The Bible begins with the creation of the world (Genesis 1)

and ends with the promise of a new heaven and a new earth (Revelation 21). These are the prologue and epilogue between which the great drama of God's self-revelation unfolds. Throughout Scripture God speaks to us through historical events interpreted by His inspired prophets and apostles.

The Bible opens with the creation narrative, given in dramatic condensation. It tells us how we came to be and about the world that surrounds us, not that nature is over man but that man is to be over nature. Man, "the masterpiece of creation," is made in the image of God. This gives to man his place, dignity, and purpose. The creation account is not only found in Genesis 1 and 2; it is echoed throughout the Old and New Testaments: Psalm 19; Proverbs 8:22-31; Matthew 19:4; Romans 1:20; Colossians 1:15-16; Hebrews 1:1-2; 11:3:

> By faith we understand that the world was created by the Word of God, so that what is seen was made out of things which do not appear.   *Hebrews 11:3*

Here we see ourselves in relation to God, to the physical universe, to human society. We learn this is God's world and that man is responsible to God for his use of the world. (Genesis 1:26-31)

Here too we have the record of man's fall into sin (Genesis 3). The account of Adam and Eve yielding to temptation is in a sense the story of every man and woman:

> Sin came into the world through one man and death through sin, and so death spread to all men because all men sinned.   *Romans 5:12*

We are sinners born of sinners. The substance of man's sin is rebellion against God. Man is constantly asserting that he wants to be his own god.

Genesis 3 gives us the most profound understanding of the human predicament. There is in every man's experience an uncanny awareness that his life is not what it ought to be. Man feels that he has lost the peace and wholeness for which life was intended. He is troubled with conflict, anxiety, insecurity, exploitation, and suffering. These are not merely the results of economic factors. They are found among all peoples, in every society, in every political economy. All human history is an illustrative commentary on these first chapters of the Bible.

In the next chapters of Genesis sin's growth is described: Cain's murder of Abel, the wickedness which brought the judgment of the Flood (Genesis 6:5-6), and the building of the Tower of Babel, which shows how mankind, wishing to deify itself, goes down in confusion and division. Chapters 1 to 11 set the stage for the rest of Scripture. They reveal man's need for God's saving action.

Genesis is the book of beginnings: of life, world, man, sin and death, man's inhumanity to man, civilization and culture, but also of God's grace, mercy, and love. (Genesis 3:15; 8:21-22; 9:8-17)

God created man for fellowship with Himself. Man's sin disrupted this fellowship. The rest of the Bible gives the unfolding story of God's initiative to restore man to full fellowship with Him through Christ.

II. The Call of a People

Beginning with Genesis 12 and continuing throughout Scripture (and to the end of time), we find God calling a people who are to carry His name and salvation into all the world. The first of these men especially called by God was Abraham. He was called away from idols to serve the living God. God promised him a son, a land, and that in him all families of the earth would be blessed (Genesis 12:1-4; 15:1-6). That promise was repeated to Isaac (Genesis 26:3), to Jacob, who was later called Israel (Genesis 28:4, 15), and to his 12 sons and their families. The 12 tribes of Jacob became known as the Children of Israel. (Genesis 11:31 — 50:26)

Abraham's call was a call to faith, for "he believed the Lord, and He reckoned it to him as righteousness" (Genesis 15:6). See also Hebrews 11:8-12. It was a call to trust in God's grace and mercy (Romans 4:1-25; Galatians 3:6-9; James 2:23). Abraham proved his faith by standing the test given when God asked him to sacrifice Isaac, the son of promise. (Genesis 22; Hebrews 11:17-19)

During a famine in Canaan Jacob's sons sought food in Egypt. There they and their families were held in bondage under oppressive Pharaohs for 430 years (Exodus 12:40-41). At this time God called a shepherd named Moses to become the deliverer of His chosen people. God made a marvelous revelation of Himself and of the needs of His people at the burning bush (Exodus 3:1-22). Moses went to Egypt. His appeals to Pharaoh and the final miraculous deliverance by opening the Red Sea are well known (Exodus 4—15). This exodus event is the chief Old Testament demonstration of God's redemptive concern, not only for the Children of Israel but for all men. It is referred to again and again throughout Scripture (Psalm 105:23-37; Deuteronomy 6:20-25). At the close of his ministry Moses reminds the Israelites that they are God's chosen people, not because of their numbers or merit but solely because God has placed His love upon them:

> You are a people holy to the Lord your God; the Lord your God has chosen you to be a people for His own possession. . . . Know therefore that the Lord your God is God, the faithful God who keeps covenant and steadfast love with those who love Him and keep His commandments.
>
> *Deuteronomy 7:6-9*

At every harvest festival Israel repeated the story of deliverance as a response to the priest:

> You shall make response before the Lord your God, "A wandering Aramean was my father; and he went down into Egypt and sojourned there, few in number; and there he became a nation, great, mighty, and populous. And the Egyptians treated us harshly and afflicted us and laid upon us hard bondage. Then we cried to the Lord the God of our fathers, and the Lord heard our voice and saw our affliction, our toil, and our oppression; and the Lord brought us out of Egypt with a mighty hand and an outstretched arm, with great terror, with signs and wonders; and He brought us into this place and gave us this land, a land flowing with milk and honey. And behold, now I bring the first of the fruit of the ground, which Thou, O Lord, hast given me." And you shall set it down before the Lord your God, and worship before the Lord your God. *Deuteronomy 26:5-10*

Also read Deuteronomy 26:16-19.

Israel's deliverance has a fourfold meaning: (1) God chose them; they did not choose God, (2) they were distinct from all others by their obedient faith, (3) God repeatedly saved them from extinction, and (4) God chose them to be a blessing to all the world. (Genesis 12:3)

The calling of Abraham is the *key* to all Christian history. (Romans 4:1-25)

III. The Covenant of God with His People

God confirmed the call by making a covenant with His chosen people. A covenant is an agreement between two or more people. After the Flood God made a covenant with Noah not to destroy humanity again (Genesis 8:21-22; 9:17). He bound Himself to Abraham and his descendants with an "everlasting covenant" (Genesis 12:3; 15:18; 17:2, 4, 7, 11, 13-14, 17) never to be annulled. (Galatians 3:17; Romans 11:28-29)

> I will establish My covenant between Me and you and your descendants after you throughout their generations for an everlasting covenant, to be God to you and to your descendants after you.
> *Genesis 17:7*

The covenant was perpetuated through a visible sign, the circumcision of all male Israelites (Genesis 17:13). Although the people fail again and again, His promise is never revoked. God is the guarantor.

The covenant is based on God's grace (Isaiah 41:8-14). Its keynote is the Hebrew word *chesed*, which is translated as lovingkindness, mercy, steadfastness, grace, steadfast love. It is the undeserved favor of God and is embraced by faith. The Israelites therefore are not a community because of their race or blood, but because of their common faith in God's promise. What happens to Israel in the course of history is not accidental; it is part of God's gracious salvation plan.

To bind His people to Himself, God gives them the Ten Commandments (Exodus 19:4-6; 20), called the tables of the covenant in Deuteronomy 9:11. He also gives them ordinances of worship,

116

sacrifices, and services. By willing obedience the believers are to demonstrate that they are the people of God. The covenant is solemnly ratified before all the people when the blood of the sacrifice is sprinkled, half of it upon the altar, half over the people. (Exodus 24:6-8)

This God-given law becomes our condemnation when it is broken (Deuteronomy 28:15; 30:15; Romans 3:19-24). It shows us our sinful situation and the need of a Savior, in whom alone our condemnation can be overcome (Galatians 3:21-29; Romans 5:6-21; 7:7-25). "The Gospel does not abolish the commandments, rather it produces in us the obedience of faith, which is the joyful response to the grace received in Christ by the power of the Holy Spirit" (deDietrich, pp. 61 – 62). Refer also to Romans 8:1-17; 12:1-2; Galatians 5:13-23. Thus we see the harmony between the Old and New Testaments. The covenant idea is fundamental to both. Christians enter into a covenant with God by means of Baptism. The covenant is understood only by faith. (2 Corinthians 3:14-16)

Though God is unfailing, Israel was unfaithful and repeatedly had to be called back to its covenant relation with Him (Amos 3; Hosea 2; Jeremiah 7; Zechariah 3:18). A new covenant, prophesied by Jeremiah, is to be written in the heart by the Holy Spirit.

> Behold, the days are coming, says the Lord, when I will make a new covenant with the house of Israel and the house of Judah, not like the covenant which I made with their fathers when I took them by the hand to bring them out of the land of Egypt, my covenant which they broke, though I was their husband, says the Lord. But this is the covenant which I will make with the house of Israel after those days, says the Lord: I will put My law within them, and I will write it upon their hearts; and I will be their God, and they shall be My people. . . . I will forgive their iniquity, and I will remember their sin no more. *Jeremiah 31:31-34*

This promise was fulfilled in the New Testament (Hebrews 8; 10:16-17). Paul regards himself a minister of the New Covenant (2 Corinthians 3:6; Hebrews 8:6; 9:11-15; 10:19, 29). Jesus is the Mediator of that New Covenant. Hebrews 12:24

God initiates the covenant, gives the commandments to show

how Israel should demonstrate its relationship to God and to man, specifies a way of forgiveness to reestablish the relationship when it is broken by sin, and teaches righteousness by grace through faith. (Genesis 15:6; Habakkuk 2:4; Psalm 31:1)

The Passover meal as first observed in Egypt, the shedding of Christ's blood on the cross for man's salvation, and the observance of the Lord's Supper as the New Covenant in our day form a single, closely connected chain of events in salvation history.

For a review of Israel's making, breaking, and renewing of the covenant read Nehemiah 9, especially verses 8, 17, 32, 38.

IV. The Priests — Worship in the Old Testament

The worship of God is assumed and illustrated everywhere in the Bible. Cain and Abel brought offerings to the Lord. Noah after the Flood built an altar to God. Abraham, in every place where he set up his tent, called his family together for worship.

One of the 12 tribes (Levi) was set aside for service in God's house. Those who ministered to the Lord were called Levites. Priests were selected from the house of Aaron. Their primary responsibility was to mediate between God and man. As custodians of the Law they were also commissioned to instruct the people. Priests and Levites went through all the cities teaching the Law and the Prophets (2 Chronicles 17:9). They also interpreted the worship in tabernacle and temple.

Israel's public worship consisted chiefly of sacrifices: gift offerings, burnt offerings, peace offerings, sin offerings, guilt offerings, meal and drink offerings. Daily offerings (morning and evening) and Sabbath and festival offerings were prescribed in detail. Most of these had redemptive or atoning significance.

> The life of the flesh is in the blood; and I have given it for you upon the altar to make atonement for your souls; for it is the blood that makes atonement, by reason of the life.
>
> *Leviticus 17:11*

On the day of atonement one animal was offered on the altar. A second was driven into the wilderness after the priest had confessed over its head the sins of the people. (Leviticus 16; Exodus 30:10)

A full schedule of festivals established a rhythm of worship: Sabbath, New Moon, Passover, Pentecost, Tabernacles. The Passover (Deuteronomy 16:1-8) commemorated Israel's deliverance from Egypt. For a summary of all appointed feasts read Leviticus 23. All of these were designed to help God's people pray, praise, and thank Him. They visualized the need of constant forgiveness and of a daily renewed relationship to God. (Genesis 2:3; Deuteronomy 5:15; Ezekiel 20:12)

A portable sanctuary, called the tabernacle, was used by the Israelites in their desert wanderings and long after their entry into Canaan. There it was set up at various points (Shiloh, Nob, Gibeon). In Solomon's day it was superseded by a magnificent temple. The furnishings of tabernacle and temple were exquisite, and the priestly garments were of the choicest materials. (Exodus 25 – 30; 35 – 40)

Old Testament worship is fully described in the Book of Leviticus. Its contents can be summarized under four headings: (1) God's holiness, (2) man's need of purification, (3) sacrifices for reconciliation with God, and (4) weekly, monthly, and special festivals. The New Testament Book of Hebrews interprets (for Christians) Israel's worship as consisting of types, symbols, and "foreshadowings" of Christ, the great High Priest. In Him the Old Testament promises and sacrifices are fulfilled and for that reason no longer necessary. (Colossians 2:16-17; Hebrews 8:5; 9:5, 9, 24; 10:1, 4, 19-22; Romans 3:23-25; 1 Peter 1:18-19; Revelation 5:9.) John the Baptizer summarized all this when he pointed to Jesus and said: "Behold, the Lamb of God, who takes away the sin of the world!" (John 1:29)

The Psalms were the hymns and prayers of God's people. The Law and the Prophets were read at certain assemblies and special convocations (Nehemiah 8:7-9, 18; Deuteronomy 31:9-13; 2 Kings 22 and 23). Synagogues came into existence 500 – 400 B. C. They were used chiefly for teaching. A portion of the Old Testament was read every Sabbath, so that during the year the whole Pentateuch (Genesis to Deuteronomy) was reread. Prophets and priests reminded the people that God did not desire mere sacrifices or religiosity but the devotion of their hearts. (Psalm 51:10-11)

Along with worship and, in fact, as a part of it was the recital of God's mighty acts of salvation. Parents and teachers rehearsed them from generation to generation. When the ark of the covenant was moved across the Jordan River, 12 stones were picked up and moved to Gilgal to be a visual aid for yet unborn children and a signal for parents to tell the story of their deliverance by God. (Joshua 4:21-24; Deuteronomy 6; Psalm 78:1-8)

V. The Kings of Judah and Israel

In the Old Testament God's people from Moses onward formed a theocracy (God was their Ruler). The descendants of Abraham were both a religious community (church) and a political state, a nation among nations. Kings, priests, and prophets were God's leaders.

Before his death Moses gave the staff of leadership to Joshua, under whom the Children of Israel crossed the Jordan after 40 years of wilderness wandering and began the conquest of the Promised Land. This story is told in the books of Numbers, Joshua, and Judges. It is a story of obedience and disobedience, of victory and defeats. God's call to faithfulness and a summary of His gracious dealings are given in Joshua 1:1-9 and 24:1-4, 14-28.

> This Book of the Law shall not depart out of your mouth, but you shall meditate on it day and night, that you may be careful to do according to all that is written in it; for then you shall make your way prosperous, and then you shall have good success. *Joshua 1:8*

To deliver His people from their enemies, God gave to these pioneers in a new land 12 "judges" or deliverers. They were men led by the Spirit of God. The two best known are Gideon and Samson. They ruled the 12 tribes for about 350 years, from the death of Joshua to the time of Samuel. The conquest of Canaan was not easy and was never complete. It was a period of confusion, turbulence, and division.

The restless people asked for a king. Samuel, considered the last of the judges and the first of the prophets, was guided to anoint Saul. Saul was a disappointment as a king. He was a usurper, taking the priestly functions into his own hands contrary to God's law. The kingship was then given to David and later to his son

Solomon. God selected the latter to build the magnificent temple in Jerusalem. Under these two kings Israel was in its period of glory.

After Solomon there was a division of the monarchy into the Northern Kingdom (10 tribes), called Israel, and the Southern Kingdom (two tribes), called Judah.

This division sprang from many causes, among them self-seeking pride, envy of pagan nations, and unfaithfulness to God's covenant. With spiritual decline came many problems in both Judah and Israel. The seceding 10 northern tribes (Israel) set up their own places of worship with semipagan rites, and some people defected to the worship of Baal.

Both Judah (south) and Israel (north) entered into treaties with their pagan neighbors (Egypt, Syria, Philistia, Assyria) and engaged in military conflicts.

Most of the kings did evil in the sight of God. The record shows intrigue, murders, revolts, and disregard for God's covenant. Joash, Hezekiah, and Josiah instituted reforms, but they were short lived (2 Kings 18:4-6; 2 Kings 22—23). During this period the prophets appeared (Samuel, Elijah, Elisha, Nathan, Amos, Jeremiah, Isaiah, etc.) to call both Israel and Judah back to God. But heedless leaders and people defied these calls. Eventually God used Assyria to conquer Israel (2 Kings 17) and Babylonia (Chaldea) to take Judah captive (2 Chronicles 36) and sack their lands.

Yet God's grace was not withdrawn. Forgiveness was assured to David by Nathan (2 Samuel 12:1-15), to cite only one example. It was Nathan also who prophesied of an everlasting kingdom — not a political kingdom but one in the hearts of men (2 Samuel 7:4, 13, 16). Jesus Christ, repeatedly called David's Son, fulfilled that prophecy. (Mark 1:15)

For an overview of the period of the kings, study the chart at the end of this book. It shows the time span covered, the years of each king's reign, the united kingdom, the divided kingdoms, the fall of Israel and the Assyrian captivity, the fall of Judah and the Babylonian captivity.

VI. The Prophets and Their Role

Because the kings no longer served God's purpose, God at

various times raised up prophets. They witnessed to king and people, calling them to repentance, to sincere faith, to loyal obedience. They announced both blessings and woes. They lived concurrently with the kings, serving in either the Southern or the Northern Kingdom or in both. (See charts.)

Who were the prophets? They were men (and a few women) called by God to declare His will to their generation, especially to leaders. They were wholly devoted "men of God," also called seers, receiving visions from God (1 Samuel 9:9; Amos 1:1; Isaiah 1:1). They were not self-appointed but called by God for their role. They were *forthtellers* who spoke the Word of God to the civil, political, and spiritual problems of their day. Occasionally they were also *foretellers* through whom God gave a prophecy of the future.

We usually think of the prophets who left written messages. The major literary prophets were Isaiah, Jeremiah, Ezekiel, and Daniel. The so-called minor prophets extended from Hosea to Malachi. Moses and Samuel were also called prophets. But there were also nonwriting prophets, such as Nathan, Gad, Shemaiah, Abijah, Elijah, Elisha, Micaiah, Obed, Miriam, Deborah, and Huldah. They likewise spoke to contemporary crises. A school of the prophets is referred to in 1 Samuel 10:5-6; 19:20.

The prophets encouraged God's people to trust only in His power and mercy, not in personal merit or human allies; to depend for physical and spiritual well-being on God's Word and faithfulness, on God's covenant and redeeming grace; and to obey God with the whole heart. They predicted future events, such as the Babylonian exile and the return of a faithful remnant. God's people were yet to fulfill their destiny, and then "they shall know that I am Jehovah." Subsequent events proved this to be true.

The prophets were called by God to proclaim the meaning of crises, to pronounce judgment, and call to repentance and faith. Thus Amos, one of the first prophets (he spoke to the Northern Kingdom, 7:7-9), exposed Israel's mere religiosity, man's inhumanity to man, and other flagrant sins, to show how far the people had fallen away from God. It was Isaiah who called Judah back to hope (53:5), giving the promise of the Suffering Servant. This prophecy is interpreted for us in the New Testament as coming to complete fulfillment in Jesus Christ. (1 Peter 2:21-25; Acts 8; 1 Corinthians 15:3)

Like searchlights the prophets exposed the wrongs of Judah and Israel. In the face of God's judgments, the people recognized their sins. Disasters are a call to repentance and to a return to God for mercy. In the prophetic writings we have Law and Gospel, judgment and mercy, a call to repentance and a call to faith. As examples examine Isaiah 1:4-6, 11, 16-18; 40:1-5; Amos 8:4-6; 9:11-12.

God's justice was exercised through King Nebuchadnezzar, who took the people of Judah out of Palestine into exile in Babylon. There they had no temple, and sacrifices ceased. While some defected, others remained faithful and yearned for the time when they could build again the walls of Zion and the temple of worship which had been destroyed (Psalm 137:1-2). Crushed beneath the heel of the conquerors, the Northern Kingdom was destroyed by the Assyrians in 722 B. C. and, 135 years later, the Southern Kingdom by the Babylonians in 587 B. C. During the time of the two kingdoms and the exile the prophets carried out their mission.

The Book of Daniel was written to give hope to the exiles in Babylon. It speaks of the eventual triumph of the children of God and reveals the true God as the Lord of history. Like Ezekiel, it is largely apocalyptic in nature, conveying its messages in symbols, visions, and rich imagery.

As the exiled Jews, by an edict of King Cyrus of Babylon, were returned to Jerusalem under Zerubbabel, they were given both political and spiritual leadership by Ezra and Nehemiah. Under the latter the walls of the city were rebuilt and the temple was reconstructed. A recital of events of this period in Nehemiah 9 calls attention to the steadfast love of God:

> They refused to obey and were not mindful of the wonders which Thou didst perform among them; but they stiffened their neck and appointed a leader to return to their bondage in Egypt. But Thou art a God ready to forgive, gracious and merciful, slow to anger and abounding in steadfast love, and didst not forsake them.   *Nehemiah 9:17*

To familiarize yourself with this period, read in sequence these chapters: Ezra 7—8; Nehemiah 8; Ezra 9—10; Nehemiah 9—10.

The northern tribes were evidently swallowed up by Assyria. However, a remnant — the Samaritans — remained.

With the work of Ezra the Old Testament writings come to a close. The assembling of the Old Testament books is usually attributed to him. There followed an intertestamental period in which the Maccabees (see the Apocrypha) came to deliver the faithful from enemies who had desecrated the temple.

During the four centuries between the Testaments, synagogue schools were developed to serve the faithful in the communities where they lived. Also during this period such groups as the scribes, Pharisees, Sadducees, and Essenes arose to reduce Israel's faith to legalism, moralism, and disciplines. This elevating of the Law almost obliterated the promises of the covenant and the mercies of God.

The Old Testament prophets had a moral and social message for their times — and for our time! Their penetrating words underscored that religion is to be lived. But they also pointed specifically to a Prophet greater than Moses.

> The Lord your God will raise up for you a Prophet like me from among you, from your brethren — Him you shall heed.
> *Deuteronomy 18:15*

This Prophet is clearly identified in the New Testament as Jesus Christ Himself. (Mark 6:4; John 6:14; Acts 3:22; 7:37)

Now take another look at the chart, noting especially the prophets and the times in which they fulfilled their roles. Examine also the line of secular history. How many of the names given can you identify?

VII. Christ the Climax

The Old Testament teaches that God controls history. Man is not the victim of fate, not a mere accident in the universe, not a pawn of the state. God is in control, and in demonstration of His holiness and mercy He guides the affairs of men and leads men of faith to salvation. While in sections of the Old Testament the kingdom of God seems to be closely related to material success and the political realm, in its essence it is the story of God as a Deliverer who comes to the rescue of man. It is not man seeking God, but God reaching out in love to man and giving His Son for man's salvation. (Isaiah 7:14; 9:6; 53)

As we look back, especially from the viewpoint of fulfillment in the New Testament, we see that our God is ever the same, a God of mercy and love. He delivers man from his human predicament. He calls a people to be a light to all nations. He announces the time when a new Israel, with the will of God in its heart, will carry on the mission begun when God called Abraham. (Genesis 12:3; Isaiah 61; Jeremiah 31:31-34; 1 Peter 2:5-10)

To get the sweep of the whole Old Testament, read such summaries as Joshua 24, Nehemiah 9, and the New Testament interpretation of these events in Acts 13:16-43. What Old Testament writers outlined is fulfilled by Jesus Christ and interpreted by the apostles. The apostle Paul puts it strikingly into a single sentence: "All the promises of God find their Yes in Him." (2 Corinthians 1:20)

NOTE: You are now ready to use the "Thumbnail Sketches of the Books of the Old Testament" (pages 149—163) as you read an individual book of the Old Testament.

FOR FURTHER STUDY

The readings suggested might have been selected from the Old Testament. Instead they are taken from the New Testament Book of Hebrews, which uniquely serves as an interpreter of the Old Testament. Note the marginal references to the Old Testament. Note also the application to Jesus and the interspersed applications to the reader.

Sunday	1:1-4 God has spoken by His Son
Hebrews	1:5-14 The Son superior to angels
1 and 2	2:1-4 So great salvation
	2:5-18 The Captain of salvation made perfect through suffering
Monday	3:1-6 Christ superior to Moses
Hebrews	3:7—4:11 A rest for God's people
3 to 4:13	4:12-13 The Word of God is alive and active

Tuesday	4:14 — 5:10 Jesus the great High Priest
Hebrews	5:11 — 6:12 Warning against falling away
4:14 to	6:13-20 God's sure promise
7:28	7:1-14 The priest Melchizedek
	7:15-28 Another Priest greater than all priests
Wednesday	8:1-13 Jesus our High Priest, the Mediator of a new covenant
Hebrews 8	9:1-22 Old Testament worship fulfilled in Christ
to 9:22	
Thursday	9:23-28 Christ's sacrifice takes away sins
Hebrews	10:1-18 The Old Testament law a model or shadow
9:23 to	of New Testament reality
10:18	
Friday	10:19-25 Let us come near to God in worship today
Hebrews	10:26-39 Remember your new position in Christ and hold fast
10:19 to	11:1-39 Examples of men and women of faith
11:39	
Saturday	12:1-11 God like a Father
Hebrews	12:12-29 Instructions and warnings
12 and	13:1-25 A life of service well pleasing to God; prayer
13	and a call to loyalty

References

deDietrich, Suzanne. *God's Unfolding Purpose*. Philadelphia: Westminster, 1960. Chapters I to VI.

Manley, G. T. *The New Bible Handbook*. Chicago: Inter-Varsity Fellowship, 1950. Pp. 77 to 114.

Chapter 11

How God Fulfilled His Covenant

God made the world and placed man in it. Man was not an accident of fate. He was the masterpiece of creation. He lived in harmony with his Creator until sin broke the happy relationship. Sin is rebellion against God and the cause for man's predicament. Yet God did not forsake man. He promised deliverance through "the Seed of a woman," Christ. God called Abraham and made him the father of all believers, sealing His promise with a covenant. Abraham became the father of God's chosen people, of kings and prophets, of a faithful remnant—the family line from which Christ came. Through specific promises, through types and sacrifices, through such events as the exodus from Egypt and restoration from exile, redemption by God's grace is taught in the Old Testament.

Were these prophetic symbols and promises fulfilled? Yes. The New Testament is witness to it.

I. The Relation Between the Covenants

The marvel of the Bible is that some 40 writers over a 1,500-year period, writing under divine guidance at different times and in various cultures, carried through one basic theme. The harmony of the Scriptures may be compared to an orchestra of 40 musicians, each contributing to a symphony under the Holy Spirit as the conductor.

Some have questioned the worth of the Old Testament. But the more we read it in the light of the New, the more we realize that Old and New Testaments are not understandable when divorced from each other. The interrelatedness of the two is clearly demonstrated by the whole Book of Hebrews.

"The Old is in the New revealed, and the New is in the Old concealed."

In his commentary on Ephesians J. Armitage Robinson says: "Only as we hold the Old Testament in our hands can we hope to interpret the New Testament, and especially the writings of Paul."

We speak of Old and New Testaments. It would be better perhaps to speak of them as the Old Covenant and the New Covenant, for Testament has a legal connotation for us today. The covenant theme runs throughout the whole Bible: The Israelites are the people of God of the Old Covenant. All believers in Jesus Christ are the people of God of the New Covenant. James refers to his Christian readers as "the twelve tribes in the Dispersion" (James 1:1). New Testament Christians are called "a chosen race, a royal priesthood, a holy nation, God's own people." (1 Peter 2:9-10)

Christ fulfilled the covenant God made with Abraham. At the birth of John the Baptist his father Zechariah, filled with the Holy Spirit, saw in the birth of our Lord the fulfillment of God's pledge "to perform the mercy promised to our fathers, and to remember His holy covenant, the oath which He swore to our father Abraham." The coming of the kingdom of Christ also marks the fulfillment of the promise "to give knowledge of salvation to His people in the forgiveness of their sins, through the tender mercy of our God." (Luke 1:72-73, 77-78)

This relationship between the two covenants continues, and Christians today, as God's chosen people in our time, are to declare the wonderful deeds of Him who called them out of darkness into His marvelous light. (1 Peter 2:9)

Throughout the New Testament there is continual reference to the Old Testament. By way of example, notice the passages quoted from the Old Testament in the verses below. Fill in the Old Testament references (as given in the marginal notes).

Matthew 1:23 _____   Luke 1:32-33 _____
            2:6 _____   1:54-55 _____
            2:15 _____   1:73 _____

II. How and Why the New Testament Came into Being

Jesus Himself left no written record of His life or teaching. The apostles after His resurrection, empowered by the Holy Spirit, went everywhere preaching the good news of salvation in Jesus

128

Christ. The essence of their message is given throughout the Book of Acts (for instance, 10:34-43).

Soon many were writing down records of the ministry of Christ. Luke specifically tells us how he came to write his account (Luke 1:1-4). He also wrote the Book of Acts (especially for his friend Theophilus) (Acts 1:1-5). The four evangelists wrote what they had "seen and heard" of Christ.

The letters were occasioned by the need to strengthen the newly founded congregations, to declare more fully the will of God, and in many cases to deal with specific situations or problems which arose in the young churches. The Book of Hebrews, for instance, was addressed to Jewish Christians to encourage them to remain faithful. It shows that Christ is the true High Priest and what the relation of the Old Testament sacrifices is to Christ's sacrifice. In Him these types and symbols were fulfilled.

How would the scattered, fledgling church be served? How would it continue in (Acts 2:42) and preserve the Good News for future generations? An authentic record was needed to pass on to "all nations" the Christian doctrine (Matthew 28:19-20). By the year A. D. 70 all the apostles but St. John had died. Without the written Word the Gospel message would have been garbled and distorted. History has proved the necessity of such a norm for the continual renewal of the church and as protection against deviant teaching. The Scripture is not only the source of the church's theology but also its judge.

Most scholars agree that the books of the New Testament were written sometime between A. D. 50 (1 Thessalonians and Mark being among the earliest to be written) and A. D. 100 (the Gospel and the Revelation of John being the latest).

III. With Christ the Kingdom Has Come

Jesus began His ministry saying: "The time is fulfilled and the kingdom of God is at hand; repent and believe in the Gospel" (Mark 1:14-15). "When the time had fully come, God sent forth His Son, born of a woman, born under the Law, to redeem those who were under the Law, so that we might receive the adoption as sons." (Galatians 4:4-5)

Christ's miracles demonstrated that the reign of God had come, and His parables described its operation (Matthew 13). Jesus distinguished sharply between a temporal kingdom (John 18:36-37) and His reign in the heart (Luke 17:20-21) and therefore over a person's whole life: body, mind, and spirit. This is the kingdom He came to establish (Luke 12:32). It is not a kingdom of law but of grace and truth. (John 1:17)

The message of Christ is called "the Gospel of the Kingdom" (Matthew 4:23). Again, "Jesus went about all the cities and villages, teaching in their synagogues and preaching the Gospel of the Kingdom and healing every disease and every infirmity" (Matthew 9:35). See also Matthew 24:14; Luke 4:43; 8:1; 16:16. To demonstrate His kingship, Jesus healed the lame, gave sight to the blind, raised the dead, stilled the waves of the sea. (Matthew 11:2-6; 15: 29-31; Luke 4:16-21; 7:11-17; Matthew 8:23-27)

The kingdom Jesus talked about is not made up of self-righteous people but of penitent sinners (Luke 18:9-14). We enter it by the new birth (John 3:3-5). Freed from the curse of sin and forgiven by His grace, we become new people. We have a new life, forgiving others as we have been forgiven, serving those in need, loving even our enemies, and forsaking what hinders our relationship to Christ (Luke 17:3-4; Mark 10:43-45; John 13:34-35; Matthew 10:37-38). Obedience in His kingdom is joyful, because it is God at work in our hearts.

Thus was fulfilled the promise of an everlasting kingdom made to David (2 Samuel 7:13, 16) and to Solomon (1 Kings 9:5). That is why Jesus so frequently is called Son of David in the New Testament. His was not the imposing political kingdom many Jews expected. But the splendor and extent of His kingdom were and are greater than that of any earthly empire in all history. Even greater will be Christ's reign at His second coming ("every knee shall bow," Philippians 2:10). Civilizations come and go. Empires rise and fall. But the kingdom of Christ continues forever.

IV. The New Age of the Spirit

Jesus gave us a Gospel of grace and a new spirit, not a theology of rules and regulations.

When Jesus came upon the scene, He indicated that the keeping of the Law was not an external compliance with its letter but an inner compliance with its spirit. Therefore He said that whoever hates his brother is a murderer, and whoever looks upon a woman in lust has committed adultery (Matthew 5:21-22, 27-28). In this way He showed that all men are sinners, that no one on the basis of his own record could ever stand before God.

The way out of man's dilemma is the grace of a forgiving God who through Jesus Christ took away our guilt and gives believers a new spirit. It is this new spirit, the gift of the Holy Spirit, that brought to the world a new age.

The Spirit promised by Jesus (John 14:16-17; 15:26-27; 16:12-15) was poured out in abundant measure on the day of Pentecost (Acts 2). Peter in his sermon showed that this was in fulfillment of the prophet Joel's words: "I will pour out My spirit on all flesh, and your sons and your daughters shall prophesy" (Acts 2:17-21; Joel 2:28-29). Thus were fulfilled also the words of Jeremiah: "This is the covenant which I will make with the house of Israel, says the Lord. I will put My law within them, and I will write it upon their hearts, and I will be their God, and they shall be My people" (Jeremiah 31:33-34). This gift gave to the church new power to fulfill its mission.

This gift of power, spectacularly fulfilled on Pentecost, the ascended Lord continues to give to all who believe in Christ. Through the Gospel we are still receiving that same Spirit (Ephesians 4:7) to carry forward our mission under the new covenant; to build each other up in the faith (1 Corinthians 12; Romans 12:6-8); and to extend Christ's kingdom. (Acts 1:8)

Having gifts that differ according to the grace given to us, let us use them: if prophecy, in proportion to our faith; if service, in our serving; he who teaches, in his teaching.
Romans 12:6-7

You shall receive power when the Holy Spirit has come upon you; and you shall be My witnesses in Jerusalem and in all Judea and Samaria and to the end of the earth.
Acts 1:8

V. The Person and Work of Christ

The New Testament is the book of Jesus Christ. It presents Him as Son of Man and Son of God, as promised Messiah and Savior of the world. It enunciates clearly the nature of the Gospel as distinctive from the commonly held "religion of laws."

Jesus taught both Law and Gospel. He interpreted the spirit of the Ten Commandments to reveal man's sinfulness. He broke with the man-made traditions that were contrary to the will of God. He attacked man's basic problems: pride, greed, self-centeredness, unbelief. As Jesus interpreted the Law, no man in honesty could say, "I have kept it all."

It is not only difficult but impossible to gain approval before God on the basis of our own moral goodness. Who among us can say that he loves God with his whole being — mind, spirit, body? Our own selfishness traps us. Not only does history give us countless examples of this, but so do also the daily newspapers and our own hatreds and prejudices (Genesis 6:5). That is why the Christian Gospel puts man's salvation on an entirely different basis than the Law, namely, on the basis of God's grace revealed in Christ. Jesus illustrated this in His conversations with the lawyer (Luke 10) and with the Samaritan woman. (John 4)

Continually Jesus called for repentance and faith (whole Gospel of John). He invited people to accept and confess Him as the Christ of God. He asked His disciples: "Who do you say that I am?" Increasingly He pointed to His suffering, death, and resurrection as the real mission of His life. (Mark 8:31; 10:33-34, 45; 13:9-10)

Many have made Jesus just another moral teacher and regard the Sermon on the Mount as central and distinctive of His teaching. This is not a true interpretation. The Sermon on the Mount (Matthew 5—7) is an explanation of what life under the Gospel and in the power of the Spirit can be as man receives a new heart.

VI. Christ Crucified — the Heart of the Gospel

The apostle Paul in 1 Corinthians 1:17—2:19 speaks of the scandal of the cross. To the Greeks it was foolishness and to the Jews a stumbling block. Not many understood that Christ had come to perform the great work of redemption with the giving of His own life.

We must distinguish between morality, religion, and Christianity. A person can be morally decent yet not believe in God. When he confesses some kind of god, we say that he has a religion or is religious. However, only when he believes in Jesus Christ as Savior can we say he is a Christian. The one-word difference between morality and religion is *God,* and the one-word difference between religion and Christianity is *grace.*

"If Christianity were only the preaching of a lofty ethic or the belief in one God or even the fatherhood of God and brotherhood of man, then you would have little difficulty with this faith. But the trouble is that Christianity proclaims the wisdom of God in what men consider foolishness, and the power of God in what men consider weakness and defeat. Take away the cross, says Paul, and there is no Gospel to proclaim. The cross is the distinctive Christian symbol of God's victory in apparent defeat." (B. W. Anderson, *The Unfolding Drama of the Bible*)

So the focus of the New Testament and, in fact, of the whole Scripture is on the suffering, death, and resurrection of our Lord. This is the big message of the New Testament. It shows what God did for His people. The key words of the New Testament are redemption, ransom, sacrifice, reconciliation, salvation. Christ is the Lamb of God that takes away the sin of the world. With His blood He makes expiation for our sins. Expiation is another term for atonement. It means making amends for wrongdoing or guilt.

> We have an Advocate with the Father, Jesus Christ the Righteous; and He is the expiation for our sins, and not for ours only but also for the sins of the whole world.
> *1 John 2:1-2*

> In this is love, not that we loved God but that He loved us and sent His Son to be the expiation for our sins.
> *1 John 4:10*

Other passages using related terms show how central this teaching is in the New Testament. (Mark 10:45; 14:24; John 1:29; 10:15; Romans 3:25; 5:19; 8:32; 1 Corinthians 5:7; 15:3; 2 Corinthians 5:14, 18-19, 21; Ephesians 5:2; Hebrews 2:9; 1 Peter 1:18; 2:24; 1 John 1:7)

VII. The New Life in Christ

Christ becomes our righteousness. As we accept Him by faith we become righteous before God. Spirit-given faith is a matter of the heart, an inner conviction. It is never merely intellectual. It is a living, life-giving, dynamic thing. In the power of the Spirit we lay off the works of the flesh; we put on the things which please God and are the outgrowth of our faith. Faith works by love. (Galatians 5:6, 13-25; Colossians 3:1-17; James 2:17)

In Christ Jesus neither circumcision nor uncircumcision is of any avail, but faith working through love.

Galatians 5:6

Faith by itself, if it has no works, is dead.   *James 2:17*

Love born out of faith is described in the classic language of 1 Corinthians 13. Love is the motif of the Christian's life. Christians are a new creation (2 Corinthians 5:17) called by God to become lights in the world by their way of life (Philippians 2:14-16), and being in Christ, they are more than conquerors. (Romans 8:31-39)

God in Christ redeemed us from sin for service, that is, for a completely new, Spirit-guided life. We live in the peace which Christ procured and have security. We also live in a new freedom from the bondage of the Law. But this is not a freedom to sin but a freedom to serve and to help (Romans 6:7, 18; Galatians 5:1, 13; 1 Peter 2:16). The Christian is saved to serve, to worship God, to witness to Christ, to be both a learner and a teacher, to help his fellowman in Christ's name, to be a partner in the fellowship of the church of Christ.

VIII. The Pinnacle of Fulfillment

John the Baptizer, like his father Zechariah (Luke 1:72-73), heralded the fulfillment of God's covenant with Abraham in the birth and life of Jesus Christ. Jesus Himself in the synagogue of Nazareth proclaimed that the Scripture (Isaiah 58 and 61) had been fulfilled in His ministry (Luke 4:18-21). Matthew's Gospel records no less than 15 "fulfillments."

Jesus said He came not to destroy but to fulfill the Law and

134

the Prophets. He not only taught their full meaning. He did much more. He bore God's judgment of sin on our behalf. The alienation between God and man was ended when Christ, the representative of all mankind, made atonement for all sin and opened the door to heaven. Romans 5 contrasts the first man (Adam), by whom sin came into the world, and Christ (called the second Adam), who overcame sin for all mankind.

When we read the New Testament, therefore, we see the mightiest of all the acts of God of which all others were preludes.

"Who, then, is Jesus Christ? He is the fulfillment of the Old Testament story. He is the new Israel, God's faithful and obedient Son, He is the guarantee that God controls our history. He is our way to life, to goodness, and to blessing. He is the promise of God made flesh and come to pass for the redemption of the world." (Paul and Elizabeth Achtemeier, *The Old Testament Roots of our Faith*)

Across the barriers of time and language the New Testament speaks to you, calls for a response in repentance and faith, and calls you to be a disciple (learner) and a "discipler" (witness).

Go therefore and make disciples of all nations, baptizing them in the name of the Father and of the Son and of the Holy Spirit, teaching them to observe all that I have commanded you; and lo, I am with you always to the close of the age. *Matthew 28:19-20*

FOR FURTHER STUDY

Sunday   The day of Pentecost ushered in a new era of the church. Relate the following passages to this event: Joel 2:28-29; Acts 2:17-21; John 14:16-17; 15:26-27; 16:12-15. How are these promises being fulfilled today?

Monday   Discover the power of the early Christians: Acts 1:8; 10:34-48; the conversion of Paul, Acts 9:1-19.

Tuesday   Get acquainted with the places (and people) to which Paul wrote some of his letters: Thessalonica, Acts 17:1-9; Corinth, Acts 18:1-21; Ephesus, Acts 19:1-21; Rome, Acts 28:11-30.

135

Wednesday	Paul's greatest letter was the one addressed to Christians at Rome. Read a few of its significant passages: Romans 1:1-27; Romans 6.
Thursday	The Lord has given gifts of the Spirit to all Christians to build His church. Are you using your gifts? Ephesians 4:7-15; Romans 12:1-13; 1 Corinthians 12:1-30.
Friday	Read about and identify (name) the five chief functions of the church: Acts 1:8; Matthew 4:10; 2 Peter 3:18; John 13:34-35; Acts 2:42.
Saturday	In what sense is the Christian a new person? 2 Corinthians 5:17-19; Colossians 3:1-17.

References

deDietrich, Suzanne. *God's Unfolding Purpose*. Philadelphia: Westminster, 1960. Pp. 251 – 270.

Introduction to the Bible, Vol. 1 of *The Layman's Bible Commentary*. Foreman, Kelly, Rhodes, Metzger, Miller. Richmond: John Knox Press, 1959.

Manley, G. T., et al. *The New Bible Handbook*. Chicago: The Inter-Varsity Fellowship, 1950. Pp. 265 – 318.

Chapter 12

Overview of the New Testament

We have learned how the Bible came to us. The Old Testament came into being over a period of 1,000 years. The New Testament books were written in the second half of the first century A. D. The covenant God made with Abraham was fulfilled in Jesus Christ. He is the key to understanding both the Old and the New Testament.

While working on an explanation of Psalm 31, Martin Luther was startled by the very first verse, which says, "In *Thy* righteousness deliver me!" Luther turned to the Epistle to the Romans to see what light it would shed on this psalm. He described his experience in the following words:

> I greatly longed to understand Paul's epistle to the Romans . . . Night and day I pondered until I saw the connection between the righteousness of God and the statement that "the just shall live by his faith." Then I grasped that the justice of God is that righteousness which through grace and sheer mercy of God justifies us through faith. Thereupon I felt myself to be reborn and to have gone through open doors into paradise. *The whole of Scripture took on a new meaning.* . . . This passage of Paul became to me a gate to heaven. If you have a true faith that Christ is your Savior, then at once you have a gracious God, for faith leads you in and opens up God's heart and will, that you should see pure grace and overflowing love. (Roland H. Bainton, *Here I Stand, A Life of Martin Luther*, p. 65)

This is how Luther discovered that Christ is the key to the Scriptures. Without Christ the Bible seems to be covered with a veil. It is He who lifts the veil from the Scripture so that we can get its correct message. (2 Corinthians 3:14-17)

Christ came to bridge the gulf between man's failure and God's holiness and righteousness. Through the New Testament runs one mighty thought: "Christ died for our sins." He bore what we should have borne. He did for us what we could never have done for ourselves.

Christ did more. He inaugurated a new order in which men and women bound in fellowship with Him live in a new relationship to God and to each other. Through Christ the way to God has been opened up. The power of evil, pain, and death may be overcome because Christ has overcome them. Christ not only opens the way to God but gives us new life. Our lives can be changed. The barriers of race and class can be broken down with the power He supplies.

The one and only way of salvation is taught in both the Old and the New Testament. It is the way of faith in the promises which God fulfilled in Christ. (Romans 3:28 – 4:13, 22-25)

I. The Four Gospels and Their Meaning

The New Testament begins with the four gospel narratives. These are not a complete biography of the life of our Lord. They are rather sample incidents which help us encounter Christ and know Him as Savior and Lord. They came into being, as Luke tells us, to preserve an orderly account and to assure Christians of the truth of the Gospel (Luke 1:1-4). Matthew and John were members of the original group of 12 chosen by our Lord. Mark and Luke were not.

There is much similarity in the several accounts, especially the first three gospels are very much alike. Some events are recorded in all four gospels and some only in one. Each gospel account contains some events not found in any of the others. This diversity is seen as you note the different beginnings of each of the gospels and the different types of closings. Each gospel has some characteristic phrases. Matthew uses "kingdom of *heaven*," Mark, Luke, and John "kingdom of *God*." Mark calls Jesus "Son of Man," but John prefers "the Word." Luke shows us that Jesus came to seek and to save the lost (ch. 15). Thus one gospel supplements the other and enriches our portrait and understanding of Jesus Christ as Son of God, Son of Man, Savior of the world.

These distinctive points of each gospel become clear when you explore the following questions: By whom was it written? To whom was it written? Why was it written? What is the content? The first three gospels are called the synoptic gospels because they give their accounts of Christ from the same point of view. They give us a picture of Christ from a similar perspective. The Gospel of John has its very own characteristics. It describes a number of Jesus' miracles, to each of which there is attached a sermon or discourse. Here we get the conversations of Jesus and an intimate picture of His relationship to His heavenly Father and to His disciples. Like an eagle it soars to greater heights to give us greater understanding.

All four gospel narratives introduce us to John the Baptist, the forerunner. Two of the gospels give us genealogies of our Lord, Matthew going back to Abraham and Luke to Adam. (Matthew's account was written with a Jewish audience in mind, while Luke evidently wrote for Roman or Greek readers.)

Then follow accounts of the birth of Jesus (except in Mark), His baptism, His teaching, healing, and witnessing ministries in Judea, Samaria, and Galilee. The kingdom parables (Matthew 13), the Sermon on the Mount (Matthew 5—7), the Sermon on the Plain (Luke 6), and His many conversations with the 12 disciples are examples of His teaching ministry. Everywhere Jesus reveals Himself as Son of God and Son of Man. Christ's teaching ministry is only a prologue to His suffering, death, and resurrection. These are the climax of the entire Scripture, not only of the New Testament. Sin has been atoned. The victory has been won. All men can have hope.

On the night in which He was betrayed our Lord instituted what we call the Lord's Supper. It is the New Testament counterpart of the Old Testament Passover meal. Jesus gathered His disciples about Him, took bread, blessed it, and gave it to them, saying: "Take eat; this is My body." He took also the cup and said: "Drink of it, all of you; for this is My blood of the covenant, which is poured out for many for the forgiveness of sins" (Matthew 26: 26-28). In this sacrament of the New Covenant the Old Covenant is confirmed, and we are assured of forgiveness solely and alone in Jesus Christ.

All four gospels emphasize the Christian's mission: "Make disciples of all nations"; "Go into all the world and preach the Gospel to the whole creation"; "As the Father has sent Me, even so I send you." Christ tells us what we are to do with the gospels. If we would read them rightly, we must meet the Person, Jesus Christ. We must learn of Him (Matthew 11:28-30). As He enlisted the early disciples, we must allow ourselves to be enlisted. As He trained them for their mission, we must allow ourselves to be trained for the continuation of His ministry in our own lives. Read the gospels with this in mind. Make it an encounter with Jesus Christ Himself.

II. The Early Church—Faith in Action

The Book of Acts was written by Luke for his friend Theophilus (Acts 1:1-5). This book gives us a detailed account of Pentecost (Acts 1 and 2) in fulfillment of Jeremiah 31 and Joel 2. Acts is the testimony of the followers of Jesus. (Acts 4:12; 10:34-43)

> There is salvation in no one else, for there is no other name under heaven given among men by which we must be saved.
> *Acts 4:12*

It sets forth their mission and ours in Acts 1:8. As the first disciples went out in ever widening circles, so we are to carry the Gospel to our enlarged world. In Acts 13:13-43 we see the apostle Paul relating Old Testament events to New Testament fulfillments. The Gospel "gets out" through us, God's people.

We may think of this book as "the continued acts of Jesus through His disciples," or we may refer to it as "the Book of the Holy Spirit," because it contains 71 references to His person and work. This book is full of action. It describes the way in which God's people respond to His action among them. This kind of action is to be continued by Christians in every age.

The ministry of Peter (Acts 1—12) is strikingly illustrated in the story of Cornelius (Acts 10). Peter himself needed to learn that the Gospel is for all men and cannot be restricted to the house of Israel (the Jews). Chapters 13—28 take us along on the three missionary journeys of the apostle Paul. As Paul enters upon one new field after another, we get a good introduction to his 13 letters. Thus, for instance, Acts 16 introduces us to the new church at Philippi to which later he wrote a letter. The story of Paul's conversion is given several times (Acts 9; 22; 26). We find his great speech at Mars' Hill in Athens in Acts 17.

The Book of Acts shows us the priesthood of all believers in operation. Spreading the Gospel was the task of every believer as he moved into every context of life and into every major area of the Mediterranean world. Victoriously the new witnesses met hardships, opposition, and persecution. This was proof positive not only that Christ had arisen but also that the church had risen to a new life. The first love and devotion of the disciples (later called Christians) is without parallel in church history (Acts 2:44-47). This shows how "the Word of the Lord grew" (Acts 6:7; 9:31; 12:24; 16:5; 19:20; 28:30). In the words of J. B. Phillips, "These men did not make acts of faith, they believed. They not merely said their prayers, they prayed."

The Book of Acts is like a breath of fresh air blowing through the church. It is the blueprint for the church of today. The church does not merely *sponsor* missions, the church *is* Christ's mission! We too are sent by Christ. In a sense we are writing our own "book of acts."

III. The Letters — Theology Expressed

Twenty-one books of the New Testament are usually called "letters." Thirteen of these are attributed to Paul; seven to James, Peter, John, and Jude. The author of the Letter to the Hebrews is not designated nor definitely known. These letters contain, we may say, the theology of the New Testament. Some of the key words are reconciliation (Romans 5:6-11), faith (Romans 3:19-28), love (2 Corinthians 5:14-15; 1 Corinthians 13).

> The love of Christ controls us, because we are convinced that One has died for all; therefore all have died. And He died for all, that those who live might live no longer for themselves but for Him who for their sake died and was raised. *2 Corinthians 5:14-15*

The epistles of the New Testament set forth the freedom of the Christian under the Gospel: freedom from sin and death and freedom for service and witness (Romans 6:6, 16-18, 20-23). In many ways these letters tell us that the Father spared not His Son but delivered Him up to redeem man (Romans 8:32). The theology they teach is always centered in Christ, the Crucified. (1 Corinthians 1:23-24; 15:3)

These letters came into existence to meet felt needs and were written to certain situations. For those who wanted to change the Gospel of free grace into a set of new laws, Paul wrote Galatians. To deal with the many problems of a pagan society (also of our own day), he authored 1 Corinthians. Sometimes key thoughts distinguish the books: "Christ the preeminent" (Colossians), "the church, the body of Christ" (Ephesians), "a working faith" (James), "the return of Christ and the last things." (1 Thessalonians, 2 Peter, Jude)

Paul especially is our great teacher. His influence can hardly be overestimated. He has given us a pattern of what the church in every age can and must do. He shows us that the Gospel is always relevant as it is applied to every situation in every age. As one scholar says, this apostle worked out the major implications of the Gospel. He spelled out the doctrine of justification by grace, through faith alone in Jesus Christ (Romans 3−5; Ephesians 2:8-9; Galatians 2:16). He pointed up the sharp difference between mere religion and Christianity, between justification by faith and an attempted self-righteousness. He showed the implications of the church as the body of Christ active in all of its members (Ephesians 4; Romans 12; 1 Corinthians 12). He outlined the character of Christian life as total commitment of body, mind, and soul (Romans 12:1-2). He gave us one of the greatest descriptions of God's eternal plan, including election by the Father, redemption by the Son, and sealing by the Holy Spirit (Ephesians 1:3-14). When we "go to school" under this teacher, we learn how much Christ means to us. (2 Corinthians 5:17)

"Salvation" is used in a number of senses in the Scripture. Sometimes it refers to the past and means that we have been justified by the atoning work of Christ (Romans 1:16). Sometimes it refers to the present and means our progressive growth in love and service (commonly called sanctification) as a result of faith (Philippians 2:12-13). Sometimes it refers to life after death and means glorification. (1 Peter 1:5)

The letters of the New Testament, in a sense, are a theological seminary where all of us should be students as long as we live.

IV. God's People Today — the Church in the World

There is a distinct relation between the Israel of the Old Testament and the people of God in the New Testament. Paul calls the church the household of God (a family) and the commonwealth of Israel (God's nation). In Galatians 3:29 the church is called Abraham's offspring; in James 1:1 the "twelve tribes" of the New Covenant. The First Letter of Peter calls Christians exiles (1 Peter 1:1), a spiritual house (2 Peter 2:5), a chosen race, a royal priesthood, a holy nation, God's own people. (1 Peter 2:9-10)

The New Testament gives us many interesting images or pictures of the church, using such metaphors as "flock and Shepherd" (John 10), "Vine and branches" (John 15), "bride and Bridegroom" (2 Corinthians 11:2). The favorite image Paul uses is "the body," of which Christ is "the Head." (Ephesians and Colossians)

The Lord has given to His church many functions. Five of them particularly are stressed: (1) the function of witnessing (Acts 1:8); (2) of worshiping (Matthew 4:10); (3) of growing in Christ — in Christian knowledge, understanding, experience, and love (2 Peter 3:18; Ephesians 4:15), (4) of ministering and serving as Jesus ministered to people (John 13:34-35; Mark 10:43-45); and (5) of Christian fellowship and partnership in the Gospel. (Acts 2:42; Philippians 1:5)

Find the significant phrase in each passage, and write it below:

1. _____
2. _____
3. _____
4. _____
5. _____

God gives His church the mission to declare His wonderful works in teaching, preaching, and acts of love and service. Paul puts the goal for the continuing growth of the christian into the words of a prayer:

> That according to the riches of His glory He [the heavenly Father] may grant you to be strengthened with might through His Spirit in the inner man; that Christ may dwell in your hearts through faith; that you, being rooted and grounded in love, may have power to comprehend with

143

all the saints what is the breadth and length and height and depth, and to know the love of Christ, which surpasses knowledge, that you may be filled with all the fullness of God.   *Ephesians 3:16-19*

The Christian community is supplied with gifts of the Holy Spirit for the mutual upbuilding of all members toward this goal of mature manhood: the stature of the fullness of Christ. We are not to remain children, but are to grow up in every way into Him who is our Head, Jesus Christ (Ephesians 4:11-16; Colossians 3: 16-17). Pastors, teachers, directors of education, parish officers, and the like are not to do our work for us, but are to equip us for the fivefold services outlined above.

V. The Triumph—to the Close of the Age

Concerning the Last Times, Jesus spoke of defections from the faith, persecutions of Christians, various disasters that would precede His return to judge all mankind and to receive the believers into the new heavens and the new earth. What Jesus predicted in Matthew 24 and 25 is described graphically in the imagery of Revelation, the New Testament book of apocalyptic literature. Like Daniel, Revelation declares the omnipotence of God. It presents its message in sometimes baffling symbols. Written for times of persecution, it is intended to assure the disheartened of the ultimate triumph of God's redemptive work. Such literature was necessary when Israel was in its Babylonian Captivity. Even today such literature supplies hope and courage whenever God's people are going through serious crises: World War II in Germany, opposition to Christianity in China, persecutions in Europe, Africa, and Asia. The Book of Revelation picks up some of the symbols of the Garden of Eden, for instance, the tree of life. Paradise Lost becomes Paradise Regained. Christ the Lord takes His Israel to Himself. The last chapter ends with the words of Jesus: "Surely I am coming soon," and the church responding: "Amen. Come, Lord Jesus!" Earlier John had said: "Then I saw a new heaven and a new earth, for the first heaven and first earth had passed away, and the sea was no more. And I saw the holy city, new Jerusalem, coming down out of heaven from God, prepared as a bride adorned for her husband; and I heard a great voice from the throne saying, 'Behold, the dwelling of God is with men. He will dwell with them, and they shall be His people, and God Himself will be with them.'" (Revelation 21:1-4)

Jesus Christ is the beginning, center, continuation, and end of all things. All history looks forward or backward upon Christ and His cross. Time is now reckoned from His birth. Men live, work, and die. Civilization progresses. Nations rise and fall. The ministry of Christ continues in His disciples to the end of time (Matthew 24:14) and toward the time when "at the name of Jesus every knee shall bow, in heaven and on earth and under the earth, and every tongue confess that Jesus Christ is Lord, to the glory of God the Father." (Philippians 2:10-11)

VI. The Hourglass of Salvation History

The hourglass is a common symbol of time as related to life. History is recorded for us in terms of great periods of time, like centuries. Unlike man, God is not restricted to time. Yet He chose to work in the events of the history of His people. This divine purpose and plan some have called "salvation history."

The hourglass in the accompanying diagram is used to show God's plan as it unfolds from Genesis to Revelation. It is divided into B. C. (before Christ) and A. D. (Anno Domini — year of our Lord — after Christ).

Diagram

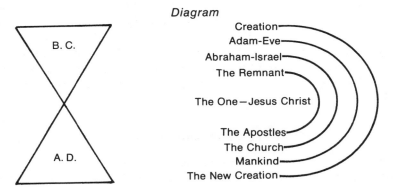

145

Note the correspondence or similarity of the general pattern in the Old Testament period (B. C.) to the yet unfinished New Testament period. The story begins with the creation of the world, which exists for the good of the first man and woman (Adam and Eve), progenitors of the whole human race. Their rebellion against God caused the human predicament of estrangement from their Creator, a condition which continues to this day. God in grace reached out to man's need and called Abraham and his descendants (Children of Israel) to become His special covenant people. But not all Israel was faithful; so the promise was renewed to the faithful remnant which carried forward the Messianic hope (Jeremiah 23:3). From this remnant, including the tribe of Benjamin, came He who is the fulfillment of the promises, namely Jesus Christ, the Messiah, Lord of the universe, Savior of the world, Hope of mankind. He in turn called 12 apostles (corresponding to the 12 tribes) and commissioned them to carry the Gospel to the world. In place of the Old Testament Israel, God called His New Testament church and gave each believer a priesthood to fulfill. The Christian's responsibility is to give the good news of salvation to all mankind, a task that will not be completed until Christ brings down the curtain of time at His return. Then will be fulfilled the promise of the New Creation predicted in Isaiah 2:1-4; Micah 4:1-4; Romans 8:18-25; 2 Peter 3:8-13; and Revelation 21 and 22.

Christ is the center of history. "To Him all the prophets bear witness that everyone who believes in Him receives forgiveness of sins through His name." (Acts 10:43)

Thus we have used both the telescope and the microscope in our approach to the Bible. To understand the minute things of God, we must first see His great plan. We need synthesis before we go into analysis. We cannot know the parts unless we first know the whole. We need to see the continental road map before we examine the maps of states, counties, and cities. This is the real beginning of Bible study.

FOR FURTHER STUDY

Sunday Examine the opening chapters of the four gospels.
Matthew 1 and 2 What differences did you find? What similarities? Enter

| Mark 1
Luke 1 and 2
John 1 | your findings in your notebook. How do they supplement one another? |

| Monday
Matthew 28
Mark 15:42
to 16:20
Luke 24
John 20 and 21 | Note the similarities and differences in the endings of the four gospels. Summarize them in your notebook. What significance do these events have for the Christian today? |

| Tuesday | Discover the keynotes of the four gospels: "kingdom," Matthew 13; "ministry or service," Mark 10:35-52; "salvation by grace for all men," Luke 15; "life in Christ," John 3; 10:7-18; 20:31. |

| Wednesday
Romans 3,
4, 5 | How does the writer develop the doctrine of justification before God (1) by grace, (2) through faith, (3) for Christ's sake? Note the supporting verses for each of these three points in your notebook. |

| Thursday
Galatians
1, 2, 3 | Underscore the verses which teach justification by faith. Compare them with findings in Romans 3—5. Note the relation to Christian life: Galatians 2:20-21. |

| Friday
1 Peter | Enter into your notebook the two most important "learnings" gained from this letter for your personal faith and life. |

| Saturday
Titus | What are the main teachings for our day in these three brief chapters? Record your findings in your notebook. |

One of the purposes of this book is to develop in the reader the basic skills for fruitful, rewarding, and enjoyable use of the Bible as part of his continuous growth in Christian discipleship. It is hoped that the student, having learned skills and established regular reading habits, will increase his gains by continuing personal and group Bible reading and study.

References

Brown, Raymond B. and Velma Darbo. *A Study of the New Testament.* Nashville, Tenn.: Broadman Press, 1965. 192 pp.

deDietrich, Suzanne. *God's Unfolding Purpose.* Philadelphia: Westminster, 1960. Pp. 151 to 270.

Hunter, A. M. *Introducing the New Testament.* Philadelphia: Westminster, 1958.

Huggenvik, Theo. *Your Key to the Bible.* Minneapolis: Augsburg, 1944.

Mayer, Herbert T. *The Books of the New Testament.* St. Louis: Concordia Publishing House, 1969. Paper. 133 pp.

Thumbnail Sketches of
THE BOOKS OF THE OLD TESTAMENT

THE PENTATEUCH (THE FIVE BOOKS)

Genesis

This first book of the Bible answers basic questions every human being asks: about the universe, man, evil, the origin of civilization, but most of all about God, the Creator (1:1, 21, 27), Redeemer (3:15, 12:1), Preserver (ch. 9), who makes a covenant with the family of Abraham to carry forward this promise of salvation. Here is the beginning of the human family as traced through the generations of Adam, Noah, Shem, Terah (Abraham's father), Ishmael, Isaac, Esau, Jacob, and Joseph. Genesis is the "stately portal to the superb structure of the Holy Scriptures." Genesis means "beginnings."

Exodus

In a time of famine Jacob's family had moved to Egypt. This book introduces Moses, the chief character, to whom God reveals Himself as the self-existent One ("I AM WHO I AM"), omnipresent, all-wise, all-powerful (Exodus 3). Moses is called to lead God's chosen people out of Egypt, where they were virtually slaves. With 10 plagues God demonstrates His power (chs. 7 – 12) to obdurate Pharaoh and miraculously emancipates His people. This is the first stage of the fulfillment of God's promise to Abraham. The Passover, a pictorial parable of sin and salvation, is instituted. (Ch. 12; 1 Corinthians 5:7; 1 Peter 1:18-19)

The chosen "family" becomes a nation, the Israelites. God gives them laws for their social, political, and religious life (chs. 20 – 40). The tabernacle, the movable house of worship, is set up. Water and manna are supplied. These (and many other incidents in the book) become symbols of Christ (1 Corinthians 10:4; John 6:35). Exodus means "going out."

Leviticus

The 12 sons of Jacob have now become the 12 tribes of Israel. Leviticus is the book of worship, sacrifices, and priesthood. Graphically it teaches God's holiness (19:2); the necessity of atonement; daily, weekly, monthly, and annual festivals for worship; and the disciplines of life always reminiscent of God's presence (19:2). Five types of offerings and eight kinds of festivals are described. The family of Aaron provides the priests, the tribe of Levi the "helpers." Some of the regulations deal with health and marriage. These Old Testament sacrifices looked forward to and were fulfilled in the sacrifice of Christ, who now is our great High Priest (Book of Hebrews). Reconciliation with God (atonement) is the key teaching (Leviticus 16; 17:11; Hebrews 9:22). Leviticus deals with the services of the Levites. It is the priest's handbook. Its key words — holiness, purification, sacrifices, festivals — all related to atonement. .

Numbers

This book deals with the training and testing of Israel in its 40-years stay in the wilderness during which the older generation (except Joshua and Caleb) died. Its name is derived from two enumerations of the people (chs. 1 and 26). It describes the people's murmurings, disloyalties, and lack of faith in God's leading (Numbers 21). It records these sins for our warning (1 Corinthians 10:1-11). This training was a necessary discipline to teach God's supremacy, His love for His people, His desire for good order, and was His way of preparing them for the occupation of the Promised Land. The book has many lessons. The cities of refuge and the brazen serpent are parable-like symbols of Christ (John 3:14; Hebrews 6:18). For a summary read Numbers 13 — 14 and Psalm 95:10-11.

Deuteronomy

The title means "second law," because here the Ten Commandments are restated (ch. 5). Moses prepares the

Israelites for the occupation of Canaan under the leadership of his successor, Joshua. He rehearses God's gracious dealings with them, frequently using the word "remember." He encourages the 12 tribes to enter Canaan confident of God's protection (1:21; 2:25; 3:2), to heed God's statutes (4:1, 5, 14), and to faithfully transmit God's Word to their children (chs. 5—6). As a motive the writer refers to God's covenant with them (7:6, 12-14, 22). Moses was a prototype of Christ (Deuteronomy 18:15-19; Acts 7:37; Acts 3:22-26). The book may be divided into six addresses: chs. 1—4; 5—28; 29—30; 31; 32; 33. The concluding chapter (by another author) tells of Moses' death on Mount Nebo. For a summary read ch. 29.

THE HISTORICAL BOOKS

Twelve books give us a record of Israel from the occupation of the Promised Land to the return from the Babylonian Captivity. The books fall roughly into three periods: (1) the confederation of the 12 tribes (Joshua, Judges, Ruth), (2) the rise, the division, and fall of the kingdom (1 and 2 Samuel; 1 and 2 Kings; 1 and 2 Chronicles), and (3) the return from captivity (Ezra, Nehemiah, Esther).

Joshua

To fulfill His covenant promise, God raised up Joshua to lead God's people into the Promised Land (Canaan). He distinguished himself by his great faith, courage, enthusiasm, and fidelity. Two spectacular events recorded are: the crossing of the Jordan on dry ground and the fall of Jericho. In various military campaigns most of the Canaanites were driven out of the land (chs. 4—12). The allocation of land to the 12 tribes is told in chs. 13—22. (In your Bible consult the map showing Canaan and the tribal allotments.) The book closes with Joshua's famous farewell addresses (chs. 23—24). For the theme read 1:3-4; for the summary, 23:14-16. *God fought their battles, won their victories, gave them the land.* Notable passages: 1:5-6, 8; 4:1-7; 24:14-28.

151

Judges

With the death of Joshua and the dispersion of the 12 tribes, leadership and unity were lost (18:1; 19:1; 21:25). The failure to completely drive out the Canaanites and the adoption of their way of life (including idolatrous practices) led to defections from God and to spiritual decay. Seven such periods are recorded, usually introduced with "did evil" (2:11, 19), followed by the Lord giving them into the hand of the oppressor (2:14), and closing with the raising up of a judge to deliver them (2:16). There were 12 such military deliverers, among them Deborah, Gideon, and Samson. Typical is the phrase, "Every man did what was right in his own eyes" (17:6; 21:25). The book divides into (1) historical introduction, 1:1 to 3:6; (2) history of the judges, 3:7 to 16:31; and (3) an appendix revealing the depth of the decline, chs. 17 – 21. Chief lesson: A nation is really weak only when it is disloyal to God!

Ruth

Set in the time of the judges, this is the beautiful, romantic story of a Moabite woman who becomes a devoted worshiper of the God of Israel, a loyal wife to Boaz, a pious Israelite, and an ancestress of King David and of our Lord (4:17; Matthew 1:5). It shows love overcoming prejudice, self-sacrifice richly rewarded, sorrow turned into joy. The book's classic passage is, "Entreat me not to leave you." (1:15-18)

1 and 2 Samuel

The story of how Israel changed from a theocracy to a monarchy and then divided into two kingdoms, Southern (Judah) and Northern (Israel), is recorded in three sets of twin books, the Books of Samuel, Kings, and Chronicles.

First Samuel gives us "biographies" of Samuel, Saul, and David. Second Samuel relates "the acts of David." Eli is the high priest. Samuel as a child is consecrated to the Lord by his mother, Hannah. He is considered the last of the judges and the first of the prophets. (Prophets now rise to prominence in guiding the Israelites.) To overcome tribal disunity and follow the pattern of surrounding nations, the people demand a king. Samuel chose Saul. The new king was a valiant warrior but disobedient to God. Because he assumed priestly powers God rejected him (1 Samuel 15). Young David is then chosen. He is richly qualified by his courage, varied abilities, and deep devotion to God (his psalms). The two books of Samuel reveal significant contrasts: between permissive Eli and consecrated Hannah, between the promising young Saul and the later impatient, ruthless Saul from whom the Spirit has departed, between David's kindness to Saul's family (Jonathan) and Saul's hatred of David, between David as "the man after God's own heart" and the man who commits adultery with Bathsheba. Great passages are: Samuel's response to the midnight voice of God (1 Samuel 3), David's encounter with Goliath (1 Samuel 17), David's confession to Nathan (2 Samuel 11), the promise of David's Greater Son, the Savior, and His everlasting kingdom (2 Samuel 7:13; Acts 13:16-23). Under David the stronghold Jebus was taken (renamed Jerusalem) and made the religious and political center of God's people.

We find here the forthright honesty of Bible history in hiding no sins (the Bible is realistic!), in issuing the warning that sin brings its own evil results, and in revealing the marvelous grace of a God who forgives gross sinners and uses them in His work. God is involved in the history of His people!

1 and 2 Kings

These books cover a period of 400 years. Chs. 1—11 of 1 Kings tell about the reign of Solomon. He strengthened the empire, built (in great splendor) the temple and the king's palace, and became famous for his wisdom. After his death the 10 northern tribes seceded and formed the Kingdom of Israel under Jeroboam. The tribes of Judah and Benjamin under Rehoboam formed the Southern Kingdom (Judah). Twenty kings reigned in Judah, 19 in Israel. (See charts at end of book.)

The story of the parallel kingdoms is told in 1 Kings 12 to 2 Kings 17, closing with the fall of the Northern Kingdom (722 B. C.). Second Kings 18:25 brings the reader to the fall of the Southern Kingdom (586 B. C.). The writer chooses to zigzag back and forth from Judah to Israel. It is a story of decline (after glory), dissension, division, defeat, and downfall; a period of self-indulgence, political intrigue, and spiritual apostasy (for instance, Ahab's evil reign, 1 Kings 20−22). Only six kings are called "good"; only two distinguished themselves by religious reforms: Hezekiah and Josiah (2 Kings 18−25). That is why God raised up the prophets (see charts) to become His spokesmen. Noteworthy are: the testimony and miracles of Elijah and Elisha (2 Kings 1−8; 17−19), Solomon's prayer for wisdom (1 Kings 3:9), and his temple dedication prayer (1 Kings 8). First Kings opens with a united nation. Second Kings closes with the divided kingdoms in captivity. God's glory had departed. Here is an object lesson for all nations today.

1 and 2 Chronicles

These books are related to the Books of Samuel and of Kings in varied ways. They repeat some of the same stories, omit much, and supplement with new materials. The building of the temple and purity of worship are more fully treated. Elements of strength in the Kingdom of Judah are featured, such as the reforms of Asa (2 Chronicles 15:1-15), Jehoshaphat (19:1-11), Hezekiah (29:2 to 31:21), and Josiah (34:2 to 35:19). Various sources of information and statistics are given. The call for national repentance is issued to Judah in 2 Chronicles 7:14, and God's efforts to reclaim Israel are summarized in 2 Chronicles 36:15-16. God did not fulfill David's desire to build the temple (1 Chronicles 17), but promised a Davidic kingdom which would be the everlasting kingdom of David's Greater Son, Jesus Christ (1 Chronicles 17:11-15; 2 Samuel 7:1-29; Psalm 88:35-36). Chief divisions: genealogies from Adam to Saul (significant in many ways for Jewish life and worship), 1 Chronicles

1−9; reign of David, chs. 10−29; reign of Solomon, 2 Chronicles 1−9; Judah after the revolt, chs. 10−36. The books close with the proclamation of Cyrus, king of Persia, allowing the return of captive Israelites to Jerusalem.

These books form a continuous narrative of postexilic history closely connected with the previous book (2 Chronicles 36:22-23; Ezra 1:1-3). Three groups of exiles return from Babylon to Palestine. About 50,000 came under Zerubbabel in 538 B. C. (Ezra 2:64-67; Nehemiah 7:7), 1,700 with Ezra in 458 B. C. (Ezra 7:6; 8:31), and a third colony under Nehemiah in 445 B. C. (Nehemiah 1: 1−2:9; 5:14). Zerubbabel rebuilt the altar, restored daily sacrifices, and began rebuilding the temple (Ezra 3 and 6). Ezra restored worship, serving as scribe and priest (Ezra 7:6, 10). Nehemiah was a patriot and statesman who gave attention to labor, economy, and organization. He finished the rebuilding of the city walls (in 52 days, Nehemiah 6:15; 12:27). Ezra and Nehemiah worked as a team (Nehemiah 8:9). The words of the Law were again read and studied (Nehemiah 8:13), confession was restored (Nehemiah 9:2), and the covenant with God renewed (Nehemiah 9:38). The deep commitment of these leaders is apparent throughout both books (Nehemiah 2:8, 20; 4:6, 14, 20-21; 5:19; 6:9; 7:5). Their work of reconstruction (social-political and religious) was hindered at times by apathy and by the enmity of the Samaritans (Ezra 9 and 10; Nehemiah 13). The two books supplement each other and refer to important documents, letters, archives, and census records. Religiously mixed marriages were opposed. Here is the record showing that God fulfilled His promises and once again "redeemed" His people and restored their land. The heads of non-Jewish empires − Cyrus, Darius, Ahasuerus, and Artaxerxes − become instruments of God to carry out His plans.

Ezra and Nehemiah

Esther	This fascinating book of 10 chapters tells the story of a beautiful Jewish orphan girl who was selected to be queen in the court of Xerxes, king of Persia, during the 80-year interval between the return of the first Jewish captives under Zerubbabel and those led back to Jerusalem by Ezra. It teaches the providence of God in a most remarkable way. Haman, the king's courtier, develops a plot for the massacre of all Jews. At the risk of her position and life Esther breaks precedent and intercedes for the life of her people, recognizing that she "had come to the kingdom for such a time as this" (4:14). Her plea saves her people, and Haman is punished with death. The book teaches that God preserves His people.

THE WISDOM AND WORSHIP LITERATURE

Job	This book is cast in dramatic form. Job is in dialog with three friends discussing the problem of suffering and misfortune. Hurt by the insinuations of his friends, he stands fast in his integrity and in his confident faith in the resurrection (19:25-27). The play is presented in prologue, epilogue, and five scenes: chs. 1–3; 4–14; 15–21; 22–31; 32–37; 38–41; 42.
Psalms	These 150 hymns and prayers of God's people were written over a period of about 1,000 years and collected into five groups: 1–41; 42–72; 73–89; 90–106; 107–150. Each group ends with "Blessed be the Lord God of Israel" or "Praise the Lord." Worship and praise are the chief themes (95, etc.). Psalms 19 and 119 are "Word of God" psalms. Some psalms become part of the Passover ritual (113–118 and 136). Many carry a Messianic promise (22). They vary in theme and reflect the depth of the believer's faith and trust. Here are prayers for every situation and occasion in a believer's life. Almost two thirds of the Old Testament quotations cited in the New Testament are from the Psalms. Hundreds of our hymns are based on them. (Consult *The Lutheran Hymnal* for examples.)

Proverbs

Ethical in nature, many of the sayings in this book are addressed to parents and youth (chs. 1—9). This wisdom of experience in picturesque language speaks to every age. Sometimes it is personified. Wisdom is contrasted with folly. Proverbs deals with the practice of our religion (3:5-6), teaching that "God is in every event" for the godly person. The keynote is "The fear of the Lord is the beginning of knowledge" (1:7; 9:10). This collection closes with a chapter on the virtuous woman (ch. 31), which in the original Hebrew is an acrostic.

Ecclesiastes

Attributed to King Solomon, this is a book of reflections on the perplexing problems of life. It is a mirror of a life which has no moorings or purpose. The wise king, after a recital of disappointments with human philosophies, advises youth: "Fear God and keep His commandments, for this is the whole duty of man" (12:13). To modern man it says: Enthrone God in your life if you would have the victory. (12:1-8)

The Song of Solomon

This is the story of a maiden who attracts the king's attention but refuses to become his wife, being faithful to the lover to whom she has pledged herself. Purity and constancy are the themes of this love story. The song is interpreted by some as an allegory of the love of Christ and His church for each other. Read 8:6-7. Psalm 45 treats the same theme.

THE MAJOR PROPHETS

Isaiah

Quoted 120 times in the New Testament, this book has been called the bridge between the Old and the New Testament because it prophesies so clearly the coming of the Messiah to deliver all men from the bondage of sin. Living under four kings in Judah, Isaiah also spoke about the moral and spiritual decline of Israel. The book contains: (1) warnings and threats against Judah and Israel (1—12); (2) historical sketches of his times (13—23); (3) prophecies of the triumph of God's people (24—39);

(4) the clearest picture of the coming Messiah as the Suffering Servant (40–57); (5) announcements of God's judgment on other nations; and (6) visions of the future glory of the church (58–66). Isaiah is rightly called the greatest of the prophets and an outstanding spiritual statesman of the Hebrew people.

Jeremiah

This prophet arose in the sixth century B. C. He loved God and country, but was rejected because he called Judah to repentance in a time of moral and spiritual bankruptcy. Jeremiah was God's spokesman when Judah was taken captive to Babylon and Jerusalem was destroyed (586 B. C.). In this time of gloom and stubborn impenitence, courageous Jeremiah gave warnings, entreaties, judgments, and glorious prophecies of the righteous remnant and of the coming of the Messianic King. He announced the covenant of grace and the turning of the nations to God. He predicted the deliverance from captivity after 70 years. The book contains biography, history, prophecy, but the events are not recorded in chronological sequence. Read Jeremiah 18:1-11 for a key. The lessons for our age are apparent.

Lamentations

These five poems by Jeremiah lamenting the fall of Jerusalem are still read once a year in Jewish synagogues. They reflect on sin and God's deliverance (4:13; 3:21-24). Note the symmetrical structure of the poems (22 verses per chapter, each verse beginning with the next letter of the Hebrew alphabet). This literary form is called an acrostic.

Ezekiel

During the Babylonian exile God called Ezekiel, a priest, to become the prophet of hope. He was called "to afflict the comfortable" and "to comfort the afflicted." (We too can be falsely comfortable in a superficial faith.) He compares the Gospel's power to streams of healing waters (ch. 47) and to a breath causing dry bones to become alive (ch. 37). He proclaims the need of repentance and a new spirit (36:26-27). His colorful visions and symbols are like

158

those in the Book of Revelation. Sin overthrows men and nations. God alone can give men a new heart!

The first six chapters describe the rise to esteem and position of youthful and devout Daniel in a strange land. The last six chapters use apocalyptic symbolism in speaking of things to come. Daniel magnifies the true God with his life, convictions, and prophetic visions. The latter include the prophecy of the kingdom of Christ (Son of Man) subduing the Babylonian, Persian, Grecian, and Roman kingdoms (ch. 7; Matthew 24:30). The chief points of emphasis are Daniel's faithfulness and the assurance that God is with His people.

THE MINOR (SHORTER) PROPHETS

At Hosea's time Israel (also called Ephraim, the Northern Kingdom), though outwardly prosperous, was decaying morally, spiritually, and politically. Against this defection God preached a unique "sermon" through Hosea. He directs the prophet to marry a prostitute who persists in a life of sin and shame. Finding her in the slave market, Hosea redeems her, forgives her, and takes her back as his wife. His words and life are a dramatic demonstration of God's love for an adulterous nation. Nowhere in Scripture is the redeeming love of God so strikingly portrayed. Read chapter 11.

This prophet speaks to Judah. A scourge of drought and a plague of locusts had devastated the land (1:4, 12). His key message is one of judgment. (The "day of the Lord" is mentioned five times.) He calls the nation to repentance (2:13) and to a decision for the Lord (2:13; 3:14). Most significant for Christians is his prophecy of the outpouring of the Spirit on the day of Pentecost (Joel 2:28-32; Acts 2:16-21). At the close he paints an idyllic word picture of the Messiah's kingdom. (3:16-19)

Amos
About 750 B. C. God called Amos, a layman (herdsman and fruit farmer, 7:14), to expose the sins of surrounding nations and the corrupt practices of his own Judah and of Israel. He chides them for their luxury, soft living, immorality, fraud in business, injustice in their courts, oppression of the poor, and sacrilegious worship (2:6-12; 5:21-24). With five warning visions (locusts, fire, plumb-line, basket of fruit, and famine of the Word) he calls Israel to repentance (chs. 7—8). Within 50 years his predictions were fulfilled. The book closes with a promise of Christ's kingdom (9:11-15; Acts 15:16-17). The chief message, so relevant to our age, is: Unless you live your religion, you have no religion.

Obadiah
This one-chapter book is about Esau's descendants in Edom who pridefully rejoiced over the destruction of Jerusalem and the fall of Judah (Jacob's descendants). Their pride went before their own downfall. Psalm 137: 7-8 refers to this. This book emphasizes the certain punishment of those who do not recognize the lordship of God. It closes with "the kingdom shall be the Lord's."

Jonah
This story (which is not about a whale) teaches signifi-cant lessons: God's concern for all people and nations, the true nature of repentance, the function of an evan-gelist who has a message to deliver, and the like. Jonah's life is a warning against prejudice, intolerance, venge-fulness, and disloyalty to God. The book has been called the great foreign missionary sermon of the Old Testa-ment. References that pick up the story are: 1:1, 4, 17; 2:10; 3:10; 4:6-8. Are we really sensitive to people? or only to things (like a plant)?

Micah
Every one of the so-called Minor Prophets contains great passages written "for our learning" and giving us warn-ing and hope. In this book note the Messianic passages in 2:12, 4:1-4, and 5:2; its great ethical teaching 6:8; the description of our compassionate, pardoning, and faith-ful God, 7:18-20. Micah delivered his message to Judah

and Israel about 735–725 B. C. He was a champion of
the common people (ch. 2). The book divides into three
speeches, each beginning with "hear." (1:2; 3:1; 6:1)

Nahum

The kings of Assyria (their capital city was Nineveh) are
frequently mentioned in the Old Testament (Isaiah 36;
37; 2 Kings 18; 19; 2 Chronicles 32). Their brutal cruelty
was unmatched, almost unbelievable. They had taken
Israel captive and were threatening Judah. In a literary
form never surpassed, the Book of Nahum portrays the
doom of Nineveh (3:1-4). It divides into eight poems:
1:2-6; 1:7-12; 1:13–2:2; 2:3-8; 2:9–3:1; 3:2-7; 3:8-13;
3:14-19. Written 150 to 200 years after Jonah, it shows
the majesty and power of an offended God (1:2-6) and
also His goodness and grace (1:7, 15; 2:2). See Romans
10:15. Nineveh was totally destroyed (612 B. C.).

Habakkuk

With Assyria (Nineveh) destroyed, Babylonia and Egypt
contended for supremacy. This prophet (608 to 598 B. C.)
invites God's judgment on Babylon and pleads with God
on behalf of His people. The book is a dialog on the
problem of evil. The prophet asks: Why does God permit evil? (1:1-4); God's reply (1:5-11); Habakkuk then
asks: What about the moral problem? (1:12-17); God's
reply (2:1-5). Then follow the five woes (2:6-20) and
a prayer-hymn (3:1-19). The book contains many noteworthy verses, but its chief message is patience and the
assurance that "the righteous shall live by his faith"
(2:4), a passage given a deeper meaning by Paul (Romans
1:17; Galatians 3:11). For Luther this was a key discovery. Also see Isaiah 26:2-3.

Zephaniah

The scene is Judah, about 630 B. C. Josiah is king.
Scythian hordes invade neighboring nations. Judah lives
in false security (1:12; 2:15). When God is ignored, a "day
of wrath" is threatened (used 14 times). Neither their
silver nor gold will deliver the offenders (1:18). How
relevant to our day! Yet another day will follow. Renewal will come after judgment, and then the conversion

of other nations (2:11; see John 4:21). That will be a festal day! (3:15-18). After the black picture of judgment comes the sunburst of Christ's reign (3:15). The whole earth is the theater of God's operation. The hymn "Day of Wrath, O Day of Mourning" is based on 1:15-16.

Haggai

Ezra 1 — 4 describes the return of the exiles from Babylon to Jerusalem under Zerubbabel. They were commissioned to rebuild the temple. But the people delayed action (1:1-11; 2:1-9) and were hindered by the Samaritans. In four addresses Haggai arouses them to this task: 1:2-15; 2:1-9; 2:10-19; 2:20-23. He tells them that the temple, as the symbol of God's dwelling, should move them (1:7; 2:9) to fruitful work. "I am with you" is the Lord's message (1:13; 2:4-5, 7, 19). The time is 520 B. C. Hebrews 12:25-29 makes a fine New Testament application of Haggai's message. The temple was finished in 516 B. C. (Ezra 5 — 6)

Zechariah

A contemporary of Haggai, this prophet encourages the returned exiles to be faithful to their mission (1:3; 6:15) with eight visions: horseman (1:7-17), four horns (1:18-21), measuring line (2:1-13), high priest and Satan (3:1-10), candlestick (4:1-14), flying scroll (5:1-4), the ephah (5:5-11), four chariots (6:1-8). Chapters 7 and 8 show that God desires obedience and mercy rather than mere fasting and ritual. Chapters 9 — 14 give us one of the clearest pictures of Christ in the Old Testament: 9:9 (Mark 11:1); 11:12 (Matthew 26:14); 12:10 (John 19:37); 13:7 (Matthew 26:31). The first and second advent of Christ are foretold. (12 — 14)

Malachi

This prophet strengthened the hand of Nehemiah, 440 to 410 B. C. The walls of Jerusalem had been rebuilt and regular services in the temple restored. In dialog form, this prophecy rebukes hollow formality, hypocrisy, robbery of God and of the poor, unfaithfulness of priests and people. (See Ezra 9 — 10, and Hebrews 13.) The people's false expectations of a "glorious outward restoration" seemed unfulfilled, and they became faithless and indifferent (1:10; 2:8). Note the self-righteous replies of the people! (1:2, 6-7, 17; 3:7-8, 13). Malachi calls them to new allegiance and purity of worship and life. He announces John the Baptist, the forerunner of Christ (3:1-2; 4:5), and refers to Christ as the Sun of righteousness. (4:1-3)

These brief sketches of the latter prophets show us how relevant their messages are for our age. We only deprive ourselves of rich spiritual values when we neglect them.

Thumbnail Sketches of
THE BOOKS OF THE NEW TESTAMENT

THE FOUR GOSPELS

Matthew

This gospel shows Jesus as the Messiah. It traces Christ back to Abraham (to whom the promise was first made), refers often to Jewish laws, quotes frequently from the Old Testament, and shows with some 17 references that it is fulfilled in Christ. It is written mainly for Jewish readers. The characteristic phrase is "kingdom of heaven" (32 times). Prominent in this gospel are: the Sermon on the Mount, the parables of the Kingdom, and the miracles Jesus performed. It emphasizes Christ's teaching ministry (7:28; 11:1; 13:53; 19:1; 26:1). This ministry we are to continue. (24:14; 28:19-20)

Mark

It is considered by many scholars as being the first gospel and probably the pattern for the others. It shows Christ as the Servant of Jehovah who gave His life as a ransom to redeem mankind. It is the shortest gospel, terse but swift-moving. A characteristic word is "immediately" ("straightway" in KJV). It is written largely for non-Jewish readers (Romans). It shows Jesus as the great Servant (Isaiah 42–53), gives us fine insights into His procedures in training the 12 disciples, and helps Christians understand their mission in the world of today. The keynote is in 10:44-45. This gospel reveals Christ as a "man of action."

Luke

The Third Gospel brings the beautiful narrative of the nativity of our Lord. The genealogy of Christ extends back to Adam, because Christ is the representative of the whole race. It shows Christ's salvation as embracing all mankind. It alone contains the parables of the Prodigal Son, the Publican and Pharisee, the Rich Man and Lazarus, and the Good Samaritan. Significant is the postresurrection appearance of Jesus to the Emmaus disciples and His reference to the fulfillment of the Old Testament (ch. 24). The emphasis is on the fullness of the forgiving grace of God in Christ. The story of Peter's call is a summons to discipleship for us today. The Third Gospel pictures Christ as the Seeker of the lost and the Savior of the lowly. In Mark and Luke Jesus is often called Son of Man.

John

The Fourth Gospel is in a class by itself. Its prologue (vv. 1-14) presents Christ as the living Word who was made flesh. His close relation to the Father is revealed at many points (John 17). This gospel emphasizes the discourses of our Lord, which are usually preceded by significant miracles. It contains the seven "I am" statements, describing Jesus as the Way, the Vine, the Light, the Door, the Good Shepherd, the Bread of life, and the Resurrection and the Life. It is the profoundest of the gospels, giving us the deepest insights into the deity of our Lord. This doctrine is reflected in many direct statements and by many implications. Salvation by faith is emphasized again and again (John 3:16, 36; 20:30-31). Everywhere Christ is presented as the Giver of life —abundant life—here and hereafter.

A HISTORICAL BOOK

The Acts of the Apostles

Written by St. Luke, this historical book begins with our Lord's ascension and His commission to the apostles to evangelize the world (1:8). It records the events of Pentecost and the outpouring of gifts for the fulfillment of that commission. The persecutions at Jerusalem drove many Christians (laity) into surrounding countries, where they witnessed to Christ. Apostolic preaching is a clear testimony to Christ and a call to repentance and faith in Him. The spread of the church and accompanying miracles are recorded. The book describes the ministry of Peter (chs. 1—12) and the three missionary journeys of Paul (chs. 13—28). Acts furnishes a good introduction to the letters of the New Testament. It has also been called the "Book of the Holy Spirit" and the "Continued Acts of Jesus in His Disciples."

THE APOSTOLIC LETTERS (EPISTLES)

Romans

Written from Corinth at the end of Paul's third missionary journey, this epistle is considered one of the most influential books in all literature. In sharpest contrast Paul describes human sinfulness (as though he were an eyewitness of life today) and man's only hope, namely, the righteousness of Christ transferred to the unrighteous by faith alone, without works of the Law (chs. 1—5). Luther called Romans the clearest Gospel of all. Six words can be used to organize its messages: condemnation, justification, sanctification, glorification, restoration, consecration. The keynote is sounded in 1:16-17.

1 and 2 Corinthians

In 1 Corinthians the apostle Paul deals with problems in the early church, especially in the pagan culture of Greece. Some of these problems are: factions in the church, sexual immorality, and husband-wife relationships. In chapter 12 he speaks of the spiritual gifts God has given to believers. They are to be applied in the upbuilding of the body of Christ, the church. Chapter 13 is the grand psalm on Christian love *(agape)*. Chapter 15 is the Bible's greatest chapter on the resurrection. It closes with the call to be steadfast and to abound in the Lord's work.

2 Corinthians speaks about the authority of the apostle as one commissioned by Christ. The keynote is: "We preach not ourselves, but Jesus Christ as Lord, with ourselves as your servants for Jesus' sake." It has several notable chapters on Christian giving as a grateful response to the grace of the Lord Jesus Christ. (Chs. 8, 9)

Is the Christian still under the Law? Galatians addresses this question. The letter has rightly been called the charter of Christian liberty. In a sense it is a capsule of the letter to the Romans. Its keynote verse is 2:16. This is Paul's clearest definition that a man is not justified by works of the Law but through faith in Jesus Christ. This book is most valuable because it shows that the Christian is free from the bondage of the Levitical law and the ordinances of the Old Testament. It also warns that this liberty must not be turned into license. It has a notable list of the fruits of the Spirit as contrasted to the works of the flesh.

Galatians

Considered one of Paul's later letters, Ephesians has been called the distilled essence of the Christian religion, the crown and climax of Pauline theology, the spiritual constitution of the Christian church. It begins with one of the finest statements of God's timeless plan for the salvation of man. It gives us our noblest goals for growth toward Christian maturity. It has the Bible's most significant statement on Christian marriage. It speaks of the unity of the church under "one Lord, one faith, one Baptism, one God and Father of us all." The characteristics of the new life in Christ are clearly outlined.

Ephesians

It has properly been called the letter of radiant faith. It shows the partnership (in the Gospel) of Paul and the Christians at Philippi. Here Paul was imprisoned on his first missionary journey, yet sang praises at midnight. The keynote of joy is carried throughout the letter. Here we see the secret of Paul's dynamic spirit: "For me to live is Christ, and to die is gain." Again, "I have learned, in whatever state I am, to be content."

Philippians

While the Letter to the Ephesians shows the nature of the church as the body of Christ, Colossians describes the glory of Christ as Head of the church. Its theme is Christ preeminent in all things. Christ is seen not only as Lord of the church but also as Lord of the universe.

Colossians

167

Like Ephesians, it calls on the Christians to "put to death those parts of you which belong to the earth" and to "put on the garments that suit God's chosen people." (3:5, 12 NEB)

1 and 2 Thessalonians

1 and 2 Thessalonians deal with the second coming of Christ. Paul uses this truth to sustain the Thessalonians' hope in the midst of persecution and to encourage them to remain "unblamable in holiness" before God. Here is found one of the most comforting passages concerning the resurrection of those who have fallen asleep in Jesus.

1 and 2 Timothy

These two epistles bring the counsel of the veteran Paul to his young recruit to carry on for Christ. "Continue," he says, "in what you have learned and have firmly believed, knowing from whom you have learned it." Again, "Preach the Word, be urgent in season and out of season, convince, rebuke, and exhort, be unfailing in patience and in teaching." He speaks about his readiness to depart if it be God's will, stating that he had fought a good fight and kept the faith. He asks Timothy to show himself an approved workman of God. Both letters contain many practical suggestions for faithful discipleship and true churchmanship (1 Timothy 4:11-16). Classic passages are: "He [Christ] was manifested in the flesh, vindicated in the Spirit, seen by angels, preached among the nations, believed on in the world, taken up in glory" (1 Timothy 3:16); "All Scripture is inspired by God and profitable for teaching, for reproof, for correction, and for training in righteousness, that the man of God may be complete, equipped for every good work." (2 Timothy 3:16-17)

Titus

Titus, another of Paul's young understudies, is called upon to hold to the faithful Word, to speak the things which befit sound doctrine, and to teach his people to adorn the doctrine of God in their daily lives. It is an appeal to fruitful living. A key passage is:

"Who [Christ] gave Himself for us to redeem us from all iniquity and to purify for Himself a people of His own who are zealous for good deeds." (Titus 2:14)

Philemon

In this letter Paul asks Philemon to take back Onesimus, his runaway slave, because he is no longer a servant but more than a servant; he is a brother beloved in the Lord. This is one of the most tactful letters ever written. Actually it teaches that before God slaves and masters are equal.

Hebrews

As a letter, Hebrews stands by itself. It draws a comparison between Old Testament symbols, types, and prophecies and New Testament fulfillments. Old Testament rites are like a scaffold which, having served its purpose, is taken down because the building now stands. The writer shows that Christ is the true High Priest whose sacrifice alone atones for sin. The letter exalts the superiority of Christ. The last chapters (11–13) encourage Christians to follow in the footsteps of Old Testament heroes of faith and remain steadfast in faith.

James

The author, usually identified as "the brother of our Lord," makes out a strong case for the activity of true faith in the life of the Christian. The keynote is found in the words: "Be doers of the Word and not hearers only, deceiving yourselves. . . . Faith by itself, if it has no works, is dead . . . Show me your faith apart from your works, and I by my works will show you my faith" (1:22; 2:17-18). It contains much excellent advice for practical Christianity in the face of problems old and new.

1 and 2 Peter, Jude

The First Letter of Peter begins with a majestic resurrection passage (1:3-7) and contains a striking statement of redemption through Christ (1:18-19). In chapter 2 we find the clearest statement of the priesthood of every believer (2:1-10) and encouragement to face trials victoriously with the all-sufficient grace of God.

The Second Epistle of Peter and the Letter of Jude have a similar theme. They warn us not to follow cunningly devised fables but to hold to the Holy Scriptures. Christians are encouraged to grow in grace and in the knowledge of their Lord and to contend earnestly for the faith once delivered to the saints.

1, 2, and 3 John

These three short Letters of St. John carry the simple but profound theology of John's Gospel, using many one-syllable words: God, truth, death, life, love, light. Through all three letters run the key words: *truth* and *love*.

AN APOCALYPTIC WRITING

Revelation

The Revelation to John forms the capstone of the canonical Scriptures. It records the visions of St. John, commonly identified as the evangelist. The letters to the seven congregations in Asia Minor (chs. 1 – 3) are full of lessons for our church today. The book's purpose is to give comfort and courage in times of persecution. It is therefore written in apocalyptic literary form. Believers could discover its meaning. Outstanding are the visions of events to come, of the ultimate victory of the church, of the return of Christ, of the last judgment. It contains vivid descriptions of heaven and triumphant songs of the saints (Revelation 19 – 22). Christ is the speaker. The church is His bride. Hope is its message. It closes with Christ's promise: "Surely I am coming soon!"

CHART OF THE OLD TESTAMENT

showing the chief characters (patriarchs, prophets, kings) and historical events
and their relationship to Near East history

The early dates in the first column up to 1400 B.C. are rounded off since they are not known with certainty. The Bible and the historical records of this period do not supply an exact chronology in the modern sense. Numbers in parentheses after the names of kings show the years of their reign. All of the prophets who have given us books are shown, but only some of the more prominent nonwriting prophets are listed. In column

4 the asterisks indicate the rulers of nearby nations whose names are mentioned in the Bible. The dates used in this chronology are taken chiefly from the article and tables by K. A. Kitchen and T. C. Mitchell in *The New Bible Dictionary*, edited by J. D. Douglas, Wm. B. Eerdmans Publishing Co, Grand Rapids, Mich., 1962, pages 212 to 223, the use of which is gratefully acknowledged.

TIME B. C.	O. T. RECORD	PROPHETS	NEAR EAST HISTORY
Before 2000	Genesis 1—11		Hammurabi, king of Babylon
2000—1850	Abraham		
1900—1750	Isaac		
1800—1700	Jacob		
1750—1650	Joseph		
1660	Jacob moves to Egypt		1570—1303 XVIII Dynasty in Egypt
1600 to Exodus	Egyptian oppression		Tuthmosis III (1515—1462)
1530—1400	Moses and Aaron	Moses	
1450 (Archaeological dating places the Exodus closer to 1280)	The Exodus		
	Forty years in the wilderness		
1400 (?)	Hebrews enter Promised Land under Joshua's leadership		Amenhotep III (1405—1368)
			Amenhotep IV (Ikhanaton) (1376—1360)

TIME B. C.	O. T. RECORD	PROPHETS	NEAR EAST HISTORY
1400 (?) —1040	Rulership under Joshua, the elders and the 12 judges ("deliverers")	Deborah	Tutenkhamon (1356—1350) 1319—1214 XIX Dynasty in Egypt Rameses I (1319—1318) Seti I (1318—1304) Rameses II (1304—1238) Merenptah (1238—1229) 1214—1193 Interregnum 1193—1085 XX Dynasty in Egypt Setnakht & Rameses III to XI
1100—1020	Eli (judge and high priest)	Samuel (judge and prophet)	
1050 1050—1011 (?) 1011—971 971—931 968	Beginning of monarchy Saul David Solomon Temple begun	Nathan Ahijah	1085—945 XXI Dynasty in Egypt Hiram of Tyre (979—945) furnishes material to build Jerusalem and the temple. 945—716 XXII Dynasty in Egypt * Shishak (Sheshonk) invades Judah (925)

Kingdom divides

JUDAH (South) 931—586	ISRAEL (North) 931—722		
Rehoboam (17 yrs.) **931—913**	Jeroboam I (22 yrs.) **931—910**		
Abijah (3)	Nadab (2)		* Benhadad of Syria invades Israel
Asa (41) **911—870**	Baasha (24)		* Zerah the Ethiopian defeated by Asa
	Elah (2)		* Hazael of Syria invades Israel
	Zimri (7 days)	Elijah	Ashurnasirpal of Assyria **(883—859)**
Jehoshaphat (25) **870—848**	Omri (12) **880—874**	Elisha	Battle of Karkar **(853).** Assyria invades Syria.
	Ahab (22) **874—853**		Ahab sends troops to the battle.
Ahaziah (1)	Ahaziah (2)		Shalmaneser III of Assyria **(859—824)**
Athaliah (6)	Jehoram (12)		
Joash (40) **835—796**	Jehu (28) **841—814**	Joel	Period of decline of Assyrian power **(824—745)**
	Jehoahaz (17)	Jonah	
Amaziah (29)	Joash (16)	Amos	
		Hosea	Israel and Judah regain lost territory.
Azariah (52) (Uzziah) **767—740** (coregent from 791)	Jeroboam II (41) **793—753**		Period of prosperity.
	Zechariah (6 mos.)		
Jotham (16) **740—732** (coregent from 750)	Shallum (1 mo.)		
	Memehem (10)		* Tiglath-pileser III of Assyria (Pul) **(745—727)**
	Pekahiah (2)	Micah	reconquers lost territory.
Ahaz (16)	Pekah (20)		New dynasty begins.
	Hoshea (9) **732—722**		

(Assyria troubles Judah and captures North)

TIME B.C.	O.T. RECORD	PROPHETS	
Hezekiah (29) 716—687 Manasseh (55)	722 — Samaria falls — people deported	Isaiah	* Shalmaneser V of Assyria (727—722) attacks Samaria 725—722 Sargon II of Assyria (722—705) * Sennacherib of Assyria (705—681) attacks Jerusalem 701 * Esarhaddon of Assyria (681—669) conquers Egypt
Amon (2) Josiah (31) 640—609			* Ashurbanipal (Osnappar) of Assyria (669—627) Nabopolassar of Babylon (626—605) revolts against Assyria 625
Johoahaz (3 mos.)		Zephaniah	Fall of Nineveh 612 Necho of Egypt (609—594)
Jehoiakim (11) Jehoiachin (3 mos.) Zedekiah (11) 597—586 586 — Jerusalem destroyed		Nahum Jeremiah Daniel Ezekiel Habakkuk (ca 600)	Judah becomes vassal to Necho 609 * Nebuchadrezzar of Babylon (605—562) Battle of Carchemish 605. Assyria destroyed. Jerusalem comes under Babylonian power Daniel and friends taken to Babylon Nebuchadrezzar destroys Jerusalem

Date	Rulers	Prophets	Events
	* Evil-Merodach of Babylon (562—560?) Neriglissar of Babylon (560—556) Nabonidus (556—539) * Belshazzar coregent with father		Seventy-year exile in Babylon
	Babylon falls to the Medes and Persians 539 Persian rule begins: * Cyrus (539—530) Cambyses (530—522) * Darius I (522—486)		
538			Return of exiles to Jerusalem under Sheshbazzar and Zerubbabel Rebuilding of temple begun
520		Haggai Zechariah	
515			Temple finished Esther, Queen of Persia
	* Xerxes I (Ahasuerus) (486—465)		
	* Artaxerxes I (465—423)		
458			Ezra returns to Jerusalem (laws collected and defined)
445		Malachi	Nehemiah comes to Jerusalem to rebuild city walls
			Close of Old Testament record

TIME B. C.	O. T. RECORD	PROPHETS	
			Darius II (423—404)
			Artaxerxes II (404—359)
			Artaxerxes III (359—338)
			Arses (338—336)
			Darius III (336—331)
			Alexander the Great invades Asia 334—323
			Alexander conquers Palestine 332
			Alexander dies 323
			Palestine under Egyptian rule
			Palestine under Syrian rule
			Maccabean Kingdom
			Pompey of Rome takes Jerusalem
			Roman rule of Palestine begins
323—198	(Apocrypha written during this intertestamental period)		
198—165			
165—63	(150 B. C.—A. D. 70, general period of the Dead Sea Scrolls)		
63			
37			Herod rules Palestine for Romans (37—4)
6 (?)	John the Baptizer born		
5 (?)	Jesus born		
4			Herod the Great dies